The Accidental Copywriter

Published By Master And Man Publishing

www.MasterAndMan.com

978-1-8380234-1-6

Copyright © 2020 by Alan Forrest Smith
All rights reserved. No part of this book may be reproduced by any mechanical, photographic, or electronic process, or in the form of an audio recording; nor may it be stored in a retrieval system, transmitted, or otherwise be copied for public or private use other than "fair
use" as brief quotations embodied in articles, reviews without prior permission of the publisher.
The author of this book does not offer any kind of life advice, action advice or directional advice. The intent of this publication is to simply share observations of life, stories of a life and the result of actions taken by an individual. The author assumes no responsibility for any action taken by the reader.

The

Accidental Copywriter

By

Alan Forrest Smith

Acknowledgements

I'd been thinking about writing this book for well over 10-years. It isn't that I put it off, I kept thinking what's the point?

Then one day I had a message from a fellow marketer named Mark Joyner. He was asking to meet up and hang out whilst visiting Manchester. That's what we did. He asked me over a steak why I hadn't done a book like this. I told him I felt marketing was rotten and filled with bad things. He prodded me and said that is why more than ever books like this are needed.

So here it is, the story of me - the Accidental Copywriter.

Thank you Mark for the nudge. Thank you Michel Fortin for everything. Thank you David Ogilvy the best dead mentor a man can have. And thank you to all the people and clients that have passed my way on this journey. And of course thank you to my wife Tamuna. She's been telling me to write this book for years. Here it is my darling.

Enjoy.

Introduction by Michel Fortin

5

When I first started out 30 years ago, I became, like Alan, a copywriter quite by accident. Clients hired me mostly to do marketing work in my early career, but a big part of that involved writing ads and sales letters.

When the Internet came around, I was tasked to write copy for websites, and the easiest way to do that was to simply convert these usually long-form sales pieces (we would typically mail out) into web pages. Around that time, I was looking for more clients. So what did I do? Being a bit of a geek and knowing how to create websites, I decided to open a forum. A discussion board for copywriters. The goal was three-fold:

To offer free critiques on pieces I came across (in the hope that the owner would hire me);

To attract other clients who lurked on the forum, saw my work, and were enticed to hire me; and,

To get other successful copywriters who joined the forum to hire me to write for them.

Little did I know how my tiny copywriters board (and my career as a copywriter) would take off. They took off like a rocket! I became so busy and overwhelmed with work that my discussion forum also became an important sourcing tool: it allowed me to see other aspiring copywriters in action, which helped me in finding, evaluating, and hiring other junior copywriters to write for me.

One of these "juniors" was Alan Forrest Smith. This funny fellow with an orange car had a certain flamboyance that was not easy to miss. Alan not only became one of my best junior copywriters but later became, in his own right, one of the world's most sought-after copywriters. And rightly so. The man is a passionate, dedicated, immensely caring individual with a shrewd business sense and a huge heart.

Most of all, he knows how to sell. In fact, here's something that Alan is just amazing at, which is quite apparent in this book as I'm sure you will discover once you read it. He reminds me of Gary Halbert. You see, Gary, whom I believe was one of the best copywriters to ever live, was immensely skilled in one specific area. It's the reason why he was such a great copywriter. And that is, he was a great storyteller. He used storytelling to connect with his audience and persuade. Or as I call it, "storyselling."

It is for that very reason that Alan is not only a great copywriter and salesperson but also a great speaker. After all, it's understandable: he knows how to tell good stories, but that's because he knows how to connect with his audience. It is that connection that I believe makes a skilled copywriter a skilled copywriter. To me, selling is not the single greatest skill in copywriting. Connecting with your audience is.

As you read this amazing book, this ability will become apparent to you. It is not only a great memoir and story in itself, but in this book you will learn so much about business, about "growing up" in the world of freelancing, and about the art and skill of selling. For example, take Alan's eight rules of business, which you will read about two-thirds into the book. These rules are not just brilliant but told in his usual Alan-esque style, where he weaves these brilliant insights into the story of his life. Absolutely amazing.

This is the Alan I know, the Alan I love, and the Alan that I, myself, learn from. He calls me a mentor, but I believe that all successful people are perpetual students as I am, and Alan has taught me more than he knows or will ever know. I learned a lot from him, and now I got to learn about him.

Beautiful book, amazing tips, and a must-read for anyone who wants to learn what it takes to make it. And by "make it," I don't necessarily mean money or fame, but to reach the goals one has set out to achieve.

You will love this book as I do.
Michel Fortin

Foreword by Mark Joyner

Founder, Chairman, and CEO of Simpleology
Punk Rock Marketing Will Save the World

When I first met the late great Gary Halbert (on everyone's short list of "the greatest copywriters in history") in South Beach we became instant close friends. As I drove him home across the MacArthur Causeway he turned to me and said, "You know, Mark. I needed this. There's something our minds don't get when we don't get to have intelligent conversations like these. It's like .... a vitamin."

But Gary and I both knew there was more to it than "intelligent conversation." Gary later confided to one of our mutual friends, "Mark and I are cut from the same cloth."

I don't know what that cloth is, but here's a clue ...

12 years later when I first met Alan Forrest Smith over grass fed rib eye steak perfection in Manchester, UK I relayed that story. Alan nodded. After 3 hours of sprawling boundless conversation we both knew. Our depleted vitamin stores had been replenished.

Gary, Alan, and I all share many things in common. We're self-taught entrepreneurs who are now quoted by formal teachers of marketing. (Hell, I dropped out of every year of school I ever attended, but now my books are marketing texts in universities around the world. Go figure.) We all started businesses because we were terrible employees. We all cared deeply about people, but couldn't give even a single hoot about what people thought about us.

Alan and I, though, share something Gary never had: punk rock youth. Gary was too old for that, but he almost certainly would have been part of "the movement" had he been the right age.

See, "punk" was a place for poor misfits to figure themselves out. That's it. Folks these days try to tag some ideological significance to the movement to make political hay. It's all bullshit. Here's how you know: Punk was home to "nazi punks" ... "straight edge punks" ... "anarchists" ... "surf punks" ... "skate punks" ... "cow punks" ... (that's right - punk rock cowboys)

Tug on anything that looks like a common ideological thread in there and the whole damn thing turns to stuffing and cloth.

The only common thread was more of a sensibility than an ideology. We didn't have much. But we tried to figure things out. We rebelled.

We "thrashed" against our problems and sometimes that resulted in creation.

The book you hold in your hands is the result of Alan thrashing relentlessly against scores of businesses and creating enormous sums of money.

See, there's a reason why academics around the world come to guys like us for answers: thrashing is, it turns out, the only way to really figure anything out. It may even be the only real way to make it through life.

So, I'm sorry to say it, but books are no substitute for thrashing. You're gonna have to thrash. Books written by guys who thrashed and won are the next best thing. So, read this book and get ready to get punk.

11

Table of Contents

Acknowledgements...4

Introduction by Michel Fortin 4

Foreword by Mark Joyner 8

Oh Bondage Up Yours 17

Posters for my punk band 'Clone Youth!'................21

Digging holes, being a punk and writing..................24

The Unemployable Punk Hairdresser.......................26

My Very First Advert - 1985.....................................28

1989 My First Brick and Mortar Business & "What's Marketing?" 30

I Had To Tell and Stop Assuming 32

My Zero Strategy Approach 35

I Made a Flyer - Here's What Happened 38

The Biker on a Beach 41

I Read a Book For The First Time 45

My Needs, My Life & The Difference 47

When the Headline is a Thought on Paper 49

I Discovered The Mind Follows a Path to Buying ...56

Converting Words for the Phone 59

Marketing Takes Huge Constant Effort 62

The Bigger Salon the Bigger Problems 64

Getting Deeper into Marketing & Writing................66

13

The Car Park and The Big Wall 70

The Little I Knew About Copy Was This 74

From Hairdresser to Writer to Whatever 78

Crazy Colin, "Who Writes Your Ads?" 80

The Accountant's Letter – More Huge Sales 83

The 47% Sales Letter...86

The Car Sales King With Half a Brain – Literally! ..89

Dave The Accountant & the Orange Beetle..............93

The Calls Kept on Coming 95

The Copywriters Board Online..................................97

FF3300 the Orange Beetle 100

Let My New Brand Be Built....................................103

It's Time Too Seriously Rethink My Career...........106

The Full Transition Into Copy Consultancy 108

I Went Back To School..111

David Ogilvy..113

Michel Fortin 116

Give Me An Hour Speaking With Jay Abraham And I'll Do It 123

35k, 50k and 50k From a Talk 125

The Fifty Grand Refund...127

Speaking Invites...129

The Business of Being a Speaker 131

The U.K.s Number One Copywriter? 134

OMG JAY CONRAD LEVINSON 136

Texas, Jay Abraham, Henry 8th & Elton John........140

Corporate Chaos and The Big Desk 143

The Famous Groucho Club in Soho 148

Cyprus Mobsters 150
Alan, You Saved Her Life 153
I Wrote My Wife Into My Life 155
Speaking And Classes … Maybe, Maybe Not........158
My Copywriters Masterclass 2005 162
Work And Not Work 165
God Had Gone 167
Opportunity Rarely Travels By Twice 169
Words and Accountability..171
My Powerhouse Three Letter System (6-steps with lift note) 173
You Must Write Daily 180
It's Broke So Offer To Fix It....................................182
My Jay Abraham Confession 185
One Client Mindset 187
Here's How I Write My Copy 190
Getting Seen..195
Business Building 199
When To Say No…! 201
Today's Copywriters 202
Wanted: Great Copywriters 204
What I Learned From Accidentally Becoming A Copywriter 206
Copy Is Conversation In Print – That's It!...............209
Life Today for The Accidental Copywriter.............213
The Only Tips I Will Offer New Copywriters 217
A Eulogy for Clayton Makepeace............................220
My Tiny Reading List...224

Mentor, Alliance or Partner with Alan Forrest Smith ... 227

Bibliography 229

Special Bonus For You 230

17

Oh Bondage Up Yours

'Oh Bondage Up Yours.' This was the title of my very first vinyl record I bought for 45 pence (U.K.). It was in orange vinyl and by a punk band called X-ray Spex. The singer's name was Poly Styrene.

I loved the insane name of the song. I loved the punk-rock anti-design sleeve. I loved day-glow orange colour. I was totally hooked! This was 1977. Looking back a lot of my life started in 1977.

Anyway …

Judging by the title of this book you'd think it's a book about copywriting. It is. It isn't. If you think I'm going to teach you how to be a copywriter, you're reading the wrong book.

But…

If you're really stuck in one place and you really think you might want to become a copywriter, I think this little book of stories will inspire you to do just that.

I used to be a hairdresser. Now I make my money writing.

I walked out of school at 15-years old with no grades of any sort and no options. So, I dug holes in the ground for three or so years and put trees into those holes.

I eventually became a hairdresser with a salon in a working class mining town in Lancashire, England. And I had to make them work.

At some point in my life, I ended up speaking on stages with Jay Abraham, Jay Conrad Levinson, and many other super-stars of the world of business, copywriting and marketing. Yeah, really!

I've also been flown around the planet at least half a dozen times to teach strategic business (something I have never been taught.)

And I've even sat with the rich and famous including well-known Hollywood stars and British TV stars. I even spent two weeks in the middle of the Amazonian jungle because of my writing adventures. I wrote some stuff that raised around $100k. I gave it away to an Amazonian fundraiser. They in turn insisted I fly to Ecuador and then into the heart of the jungle to see how this was being spent. I went, I loved it, it was crazy!

I've even sat in with some of the U.K.s biggest corporate companies and have been asked to give advice, tear down internal marketing teams and rebuild them into small power-houses. Crazy stuff!

And I started doing that whilst I was still a full-time working hairdresser.

I've had no formal copywriting training or ever taken a course in my life. I've had no paid living mentors to guide me. I never paid more than I should for any book on the subject. I never once read a book from start to end on copy. I just read what I needed to know to get the job done. That's never changed.

I want you to know this. I'm not the incredible John Caples. I truly wish I was David Ogilvy. I am nowhere near as good as copywriters like the brilliant self-styled antagonist copywriter Clayton Makepeace or the gentle Michel Fortin.

I'm just an accidental copywriter. I fell into the whole thing. I had no idea what copy was or even what I was doing. I just write stuff. And I suppose I took the time to think about what I wanted to say. I then wrote down what I was thinking. Sometimes it makes sense. Sometimes it doesn't. But when it does make sense every word can carry some kind of weird hypnotic power that gets readers to react or respond.

I'm still not sure how I do it, but I still do it.

And at heart I'm an old punk finding his way in life but seems to have found his way so many times it can read pretty hard to believe.

And one more little fact. I started writing Ads for my businesses in 1985. I had never heard of the term 'copywriting' until the late 90s at the earliest.

All I knew was that little punk track got my attention with its title and cover. That's what I had to do with my ads. Get attention and encourage the reader to act.

For a self-employed guy like myself I had no option - it had to work despite what little I knew; it just had to work. I wanted out of hairdressing at some point and copywriting was just one option that seemed to work.

So here are a handful of tales and stories as I remember them. I hope you enjoy and feel inspired at some level if you are thinking about entering into the world of copywriting.

Are you ready to read some ridiculous and sometimes outrageous, but true stories of the accidental copywriter?

OK, here goes.

Posters for my punk band 'Clone Youth!'

It was 1979 and England was a socialist-driven mess. We'd all dropped out of school to be in a band. I didn't fail my exams because I didn't take a single one. I just walked out from school at 15-years old. I was the singer (obviously I got the girls) and also the rhythm guitarist that really couldn't play guitar.

When my band was ready to gig someone had to create the posters for the band. No one wanted to do it, so despite having no idea what I was doing, I created the posters.

At that time I used to go to a basement punk club on Liverpool's famous Matthew Street called Eric's. Eric's was the place every punk band wanted to play. You name a 70s punk band, I saw them in Eric's.

The posters for the bands always said, 'Eric's Presents', The Clash or whoever. I thought it looked and sounded so cool. I also knew if it packed out the club for them I should copy it. That's exactly what I did.

I wanted my little punk band to look and feel as huge as The Clash despite us being just four kids in the village. So, I created the posters.

The band was called 'Clone Youth.' At the top of the poster it said… 'Blank Faces Presents' because the posters at Eric said 'Erics Presents.' Blank Faces of course didn't exist I just thought it looked cool and sounded big.

Looking back this was one of my early intros into writing words and using them to get a result of some kind. From that day forward I was the poster maker for the band as well as the lyricist and singer.

I wanted my lyrics (words) to make people think. My actual lyrics like, 'the air we breathe, the things we smell, this isn't heaven, this isn't hell, this is our world, the place we live, to help pollute so much we give.'

I wanted the words to be heard. I wanted listeners to react and respond. I wanted them to feel they could do more and pollute less. Yet these were all just words; or were they? Would the words from lyrics like this get a reaction? I was hoping so.

From that point I always wrote song lyrics and poetry but rarely showed anyone what I was writing. I was just a punk rock kid doing his own thing and trying to figure out the world.

I started noticing words everywhere. The race to stop nuclear destruction was on. CND (Campaign For Nuclear Disarmament) had the posters and the slogans with strong images. Rock Against Racism (R.A.R) was also huge. Again I loved the messages and felt their effect on my thinking. And then the mighty campaign for AIDS arrived and scared me to death. And finally the terrifying Protect and Survive campaign. (All these ads are on YouTube)

I also started noticing the words on T-shirts. I began to wear T-shirts I would hide from my parents. I had a T-shirt with the word 'bollocks' on. I also had another with strong red star communist imagery of Stalin and words. I even had a T-shirt with a huge swastika overlaid with the word destroy.

The truth is they meant little to me outside a rebellious teenage approach yet the single words alone had a huge impact. It was revolution through words. It was also a subtle mind manipulation of a young fresh mind ready to absorb. My life on those days was about words based on punk driven messages that were grabbing my attention.

Just to really show the power on the young mind, today I can easily repeat most lyrics from all of those early 70s punk tracks. The embedding behaviour of words had taken root early. And of course I only really realise this with the gift of hindsight.

Digging holes, being a punk and writing

What I didn't mention before was during the punk rock phase I was also the appointed hair cutter and colourist despite having zero training. My mum used to cut all of her friends hair at home. So I just copied what she did in front of me on my mates.

My first real job was as a landscape gardener. I'd spent some three-plus years as a gardener. But wanted to use what I felt good at. I'd learnt a lot during my punk haircutting days and was still cutting hair. So I decided to attend hairdressing college and train properly. That was 1980.

I hated Hairdressing College; it was way too restrictive for me. It was all about trying to give people a great haircut and they would pay me for that. College covered zero on how to be a great businessman or how to create amazing haircuts. The whole thing focused more on the theory. I kind of understood I had to do it, but I really wanted to just get my teeth into the haircuts and make some money.

In 1982 I got my first stylist job in a salon in Bolton, England and got fired (thankfully.) I was told I was too creative after using slivers of glass to do a haircut! I got my second salon job in Warrington, England and once again got fired for colouring my hair bright red (unbelievable) and refusing to wear a uniform. I got more jobs in more salons and kept getting fired. Something was telling me something about working for myself. That is what I eventually did because I had too.

At that time I bumped into an old pal from school named John (named changed.) I hadn't seen him for over six years. He told me that he had built a business with his father turning over a couple of million selling rejected women's underwear from big brands! Knickers!

I couldn't believe it; he was more of a dropout than I was. He was selling high-end underwear with slight flaws. The demand for the brand was huge, but the majority couldn't or wouldn't pay the regular price. He found a way around it and gave buyers what they were ready to buy. Same product with tiny flaws on microscopic things like stitching. It got me thinking for the very first time about numbers and that is something I am no big fan of especially – big numbers. (This will be relevant later as you'll see.)

The Unemployable Punk Hairdresser

I was now a hairdresser. It was 1985 and everyone seemed to hate Thatcher in power, but everyone loved the idea of owning their own home. People never know what they want.

I had been fired once again for my rebellious punk rock behaviour in hairdressing salons where I was now a high-demand hair stylist.

Despite it being common in all salons I still refused to wear the salon uniform. My hair was bright red and purple. My jeans were ripped and shredded. I wore a T-shirt with a message so obscene that I refuse to write it here now. The uniform was plain black like a waiter waiting for nothing to happen.

Anyway, I got fired despite being the busiest hairdresser they ever had up until that point. So, in 1985 I decided it would be better working on my own rather than being fired for being a rule-breaking non-conformist. I wanted to break the rules. I wanted to do my own thing. My power had come from words.

So during the first week of December 1985 I was fired from my very last place of employment. I drove home furious, but relieved.

27

My Very First Advert - 1985

I had to write a small ad.

I'd been fired again and I needed money. I had clients, but they just needed to know how to get hold of me.

I thought about it and decided that if I put a small advert in the newspaper my clients would see the advert and call me. I did just that and the clients called. This was the very first time I had created an advert for any business.

I gave the advert absolutely zero thought. All I knew was the clients knew my name, my face and probably wanted to know where I was now.

I put a 'prison-like' passport photo on the advert that said… 'Alan the hairdresser can be found here…' I added my landline and voicemail number. That was it.

I was out all day cutting the nurses hair at the hospital (long story, but my mother worked there and would gather half a dozen together so I could cut their hair in a disused operating theatre.)

When I got home in the evening I totally shocked. The C-30 cassette that took my voicemail was ram-jam-full with clients wanting hair appointments from that small ad.

My name (headline) and the photo (meme) told them who and where I was. The call to action (take a direct response) was the phone number. It worked.

I ran that tiny advert without the photo in classifieds for the next 4-years until 1989 and my phone and voicemail never stopped ringing. 1989 is the year when I decided to 'accidentally' open my first brick and mortar business.

Something even more radical happened in my life in this period. first, I bought my very first house. Second … In 1985 I began intensive Bible study. In the June of 1987 had become a fully ordained fundamentalist Christian minister.

That's a whole new book in itself!

Anyway …

1989 My First Brick and Mortar Business & "What's Marketing?"

I had never been short of work since getting fired for the very last time. My phone voice mail (mobile A.D.) when I got home at night was always packed with regular and new clients wanting to book a hair appointment. I loved it, I hated it, but I was cash loaded. This little ad enabled me to buy all of my early home furniture for cash and made me cash rich at many levels.

Going back a little to 1986. I bought a house, new everything, and had money to spend on whatever I wanted. Everything felt good because I was filling a demand for a good hairdresser. The demand really meant that the buyer – the client - had already bought their next hairstyle in their head. I just had to show them I had what they wanted to pay for. Once they knew of me, they got what they wanted and I got paid.

Forward again to 1989. One day I was doing a bunch of family haircut's in a client's kitchen. He owned the local newsagent shop. The client asked me if I would be interested in opening a salon. 'Maybe' I instinctively replied. He then excitedly showed me his shopping mall blueprints. His shops hadn't been built at this point. He told me I could have the one at the front (to persuade me) so passing trade would see my little salon easily.

Peter (name changed) was pretty persuasive to say the least. After the conversation and my unsure response he arrived at my home the very same day in the evening with something I had never seen before. It was called a lease. He handed it to me, spent a long time once again persuading me. Then went away so I could read the lease alone in my own time.

The lease was a single piece of paper and that paper needed a signature. I didn't read it, I just agreed that it sounded cool and I would do it. After all I had gotten sick of driving around in my car and my pal John who had been making fortune-selling women's underwear had got me thinking about bigger things. A shop felt the way forward.

I was about to discover things in life rarely go as planned.

I Had To Tell and Stop Assuming

Now I have to tell you, at this point, I had no idea about putting a salon together. And I certainly had never heard a single thing about this thing called marketing or promotions.

I'd been running a mobile hairdressing business purely on demand. That was me, a car and clients booking appointments.

I'd really had enough. One day I was late for mrs. Jones at 4:30pm on a Saturday. I had to drive faster than usual to make sure I got there as she would always have plenty to say I was late.

A long maroon Volvo had been driving at around 30 m.p.h for so long I was getting later and later. Just after a bend on a long stretch of road, I decided to overtake. He also decided to go faster to stop me overtaking. Eventually we got to the next bend and we were side-by-side. I couldn't get in front of him. Another car came flying around the corner facing me head-on. I had to swerve, my car span out of control and then left the ground, flew through a fence and landed in a pond. I had been driving at 70 m.p.h when this happened. I escaped without even a scratch. The car was a wreck.

I was very lucky to be alive. I'd had enough of the kind of working.

But back to this new shop.

I didn't realise I would have to attract or pull buyers into a brick and mortar business. I actually thought it would be as easy as you opened the doors and the clients just arrived. They didn't.

That is the time I discovered client loyalty isn't really what we think it is. It isn't. Hardly any of my older clients came to support me in the shop. They just liked having their hair done at home.

But I was already making a ton of money mobile and that money had started to be thrown at me. I honestly thought a shop should make me rich!

First, the shop had to be built. I went to see the land. It was an old supermarket that had closed and was being rebuilt and divided into eight small units.

Actually, I did my first interview for staff on that building site. She and her father sat on a pile of bricks whilst I sat on a pile of wood. Incredibly she accepted the job and went on to work for me for seven years. Thank you Kerry Dawson.

Anyway, once the units were built, my allocated salon space was very small at around 250 sq. ft. It was a unit with one glass wall facing into a small mall. My salon was at the front of the mall with my salon door facing the front door where people entered into the mall, but you couldn't see my salon from the street.

The village where the salon was based in Cheshire, England had a population of just over 3,500 with seven other hair salons. All of the salons had been there over twenty years. One had been there since the very early 1960s. They always hated my salon and someone would do strange things to my salon and me (like super-glue my locks or burst my car tyres). I had no time for them, I just wanted to succeed in my own little punk rock way.

Failure was never an option despite their moronic actions. I didn't overthink anything at that time. I just thought I would be bigger and busier in a shop.

I had no money to fit out my shop but I did have a decent little car that I could sell. I sold my car for around £5,000 (Ford XR-2) and used the cash to fit out my new little salon. I managed to fit everything in apart from the back room and also one sink I couldn't afford to plumb in. Apart from that I was ready to punk rock 'n' roll!

I opened the salon - The Big Scissor Company - on May 15th 1989. It was an exciting year for me as my first child was also due. Money was good, I had my own tiny home and now I had a new venture to chase.

Here we go!

My Zero Strategy Approach

I didn't have a clue!

I knew all of the local haircut prices. So I set my prices roughly the same as everyone else. I mean that's how it's done right? I can tell you the exact price. The price was £6.95 for a ladies cut and blow dry. It was 1989, but it was still pretty low.

Once I opened there really nothing that special about my salon. It was new and it had me, but apart from it was nothing in particular apart from I still played punk music in the shop. That was in days whilst most played throw-away pop or the Bee Gees!

I believed what most hairdressers believe and it was this; my skills and being good with my skills would be enough to pack out my salon. I was about to learn the very hard way. It just wasn't enough to bring in clients, as you'll see.

On the day of opening, morning of May 15[th,] I drove down to my salon in the 1972 cream coloured Austin Mini I had bought for just £200 after selling my little sports car to pay for the salon. I parked outside. The mall was brand new; it had no signage and had no promotions before my salon opened. I was ready to kill it.

36

I walked in to the salon on my own. I was ready to take over the world. Honestly, I was thinking I'm about to be rich.

I had not a single client booked in.

Eventually after 8-long-hours I had one guy named Mark walk in and have a haircut. After eight hours stuck in my new salon I had just £4.50 in the drawer. Utterly deflating!

The next day was the same. And so was the next and the next. The weekend was busy and my old clients were also slowly starting to come in. Clearly I had a huge problem very early and I needed to solve that problem, otherwise no one would be eating anything!

Maybe the correct way to say it is… "I'm screwed!"

I actually thought I had done everything right. Great looking shop, good skills, good services and my prices seemed more than fair. It wasn't good enough and my lack of results began to show very fast.

I hadn't made a single announcement to the public about my new salon at this stage - not one!

Even worse; the sales reps had discovered my salon and had also found out how naïve I was (perfect prey.) I think they call it an easy sell. They told me the more stock I have on display would increase my business. I bought into it. It didn't. My invoices were building and building fast!

Obviously, I started to panic. I knew something had to be done and done as quickly as possible or I was going to be completely sunk!

My strategy of having no strategy was quickly becoming a strategic and impending disaster.

Someone said try this.

I Made a Flyer - Here's What Happened

An old neighbour (Mrs. Gee who had been my French teacher at school) was asking me about my new salon. I was telling her my problems and she told me to create a flyer. I had no idea what a flyer was so I had to ask her what she meant. She told me it was like this and that and I should write it, print it, and then post around the village.

Good idea I thought. So …

I walked over to 'scouse' Jim's the local printer. I explained to him my salon was dead and I needed his help. He asked had I created it? I didn't realise I was supposed to take to him the finished idea. I was asking a printer what to do. He explained that I have to create it and he will print it.

He told me it would be 3-4 weeks for the flyer to be printed. This was pretty normal in those days. I asked him for some ideas what to write and he gave me an example of some flyers from a carpet shop. He said something like that, but for your salon. That sounded easy enough.

So, I went away and wrote a flyer like the carpet flyer. I took it back over to him and four weeks later it came back to me printed. I liked it, but it was very standard like all salon flyers. Dull. Boring. Not punk rock like my band posters. My bills were mounting fast.

The name of my salon went at the top - The Big Scissor Company. A stock photo of a pretty girl somewhere further down. My salon address and a new client offer of 25% off a £6.95 haircut. Looking back it wasn't great (pathetic really), but here's what happened. I was shocked. I felt excited to do more.

I walked around my little village on my own with my 3000 flyers. I pushed them through most letter boxes and then went back to my salon. When I arrived on Tuesday to open the door I got a huge surprise.

The salon voicemail was filled and couldn't take any more messages. The phone was ringing as I opened the door and suddenly my salon was busy. Exciting!

Everyone called my salon from that terrible little flyer. Terrible, but it definitely worked. I had just created my first real marketing campaign and didn't know it.

I had also just discovered something that I found out later to be called 'promotions' or 'marketing' and it seemed to work. So I did more flyers and kept hand posting them until I was busy most of the time and had no time to post them.

I dd try al the usual routes also. I even bought novelty key-fobs, mugs with the salon name on and other daft stuff. Nothing worked like the flyers - nothing!

I would say the flyer was the only marketing or promotion I was doing; apart from that I also used business cards and letterhead paper (although I hadn't a clue what I was supposed to do with.) All I knew was I was told that a business should have them so I had them. It was standard; letterheads, cards, and a flyer or two.

During all of this I was still thinking about my pal who had now sold his underwear business and jumped into the mobile phone business. This was still 1989. He has signed a deal in Russia that made him a millionaire overnight. I wanted more than my village shop but it was going to take more. One day when he came into the salon he brought me a gift for a haircut. It was a Nokia flip phone. It was also my first mobile phone. No one really had them. I always left it out for clients to see as a talking point. I still have the very same first mobile number today.

But like my pal, I probably needed Russians at this stage to make me rich, but realised I would have to stick to the local population for now.

This next discovery was about to change everything.

The Biker on a Beach

Something had to change. I was doing ok, but not amazing. I wanted to do amazing.

I'd now discovered ads and words worked big time for my business after my flyer experience, but I wasn't sure how to write them. Books on copy writing were few and far between in those days. And also, I didn't know it was called writing copy or copy writing. To me at this point it was just the right or wrong words on a flyer. They worked or they didn't work.

One day in the hairdressing journal I saw an advert for Paul Mitchell Salon Products. It looked like nothing I was seeing anywhere in the hair and beauty industry magazines and I mean nothing.

It was a long-haired biker-bearded guy on a beach in leather pants with a long-haired stunning blonde-haired woman. They were next to a red-hot Harley Davidson. The whole look and feel attracted and sucked me into the ad.

It never really spoke about shampoo or hair product, it just felt more about lifestyle - my lifestyle. It was rock and roll and it felt like me. Kind of like the punk record cover from X-ray Spex and other punk bands. Different, rule-breaking and I wanted in.

I will never forget the headline. The headline read…

"Cheap Hairdressing Makes As Much Sense As Cheap Medicine"

It was just brilliant. I personally had never seen anything like it in the world of hairdressing ads. No stock photos and emphasis on the brand. This was pure genius to my eyes and a catalyst for something.

I thought I can copy this type advert and make my salon ads look similar. Breaking rules, doing things different. I wanted that. I also realised that Paul Mitchell was using different words from anyone else so how could I do that with my words in my flyers or adverts?

At the same time Paul Mitchell were offering a training camp in London. This was teaching salon owners like myself how to create marketing and get busy, but with a twist. And it wasn't cheap, I couldn't afford it, but I decided to go. I stuck it on a credit card.

I spent £2,000 on the training and hotel fees and went and had my eyes opened. The meeting took place in the owners home. It was just amazing. The guy from Paul Mitchell John Paul Dejoria (same guy in the ad) was there and I was blown away.

I do want to acknowledge those guys; thank you Paul Mitchell, Leslie Spears, Di and Mike Kimble and early 365 salon owners club, and here is why.

My eyes had been opened to a different way of creating a business. This was a very different approach to what I had literally been playing at. They opened my mind to new thinking and new directions. I stuck with this new club for around 18-months, but honestly being in a club wasn't my thing so I eventually dropped out. It was worth every penny that went onto my credit card.

This was the very first time I realised that the way words are used, said, written can actually make a huge impact in turning my salon into a real business.

The words I used in my promotions could, would, and did make a huge difference between someone picking up the phone and not picking up the phone. I had to look and appear better than my competition.

Not only words but also presentation of the words can increase or decrease my response. Not just presentation of the words, but images that are created to invite response that surrounded the words. Not only visible image, but mental images also. I was amazed!

And then there was a perceptive value. How would the reader of the words and images build their mental perception of my business from what I had said in my words and presented in image form?

Now, I am the first to admit I didn't really get it at the time, but I realised there was something very powerful to all of this. When I got back home I collected and studied the adverts from Paul Mitchell and used them to model my own ads – or flyers.

Paul Mitchell were doing something so cool, and doing something (and still are amazing trailblazers in a copy-cat industry) that no other company in the hair salon business had been doing to me and it was this.

They demanded my attention and got it.

They made me think I was buying a new life. They made me think I was in business to build a life, not just building a successful business. My core need was being addressed through Paul Mitchell ads and that core need was this;

'Alan, you want to have all the good things in life and create a lifestyle that makes you feel good? Selling our stuff in your salon gives you that.'

Get this again: I wasn't building a business I was building a life. The business was simply a tool to build my life in those days.

Next came the books.

I Read a Book For The First Time

Now, I'm not proud of saying this.

But up until this age in my life I had never read any books (I had begun reading and studying the Bible from 1985 onwards). That was just a fact. And that was the ONLY book.

But at this business club I had also seen books of curiosity for sale. I saw them, poured over them, and bought my very first business books at this salon club.

One by Tom Peters, another by Zig Ziglar, one from a guy named Michel Le Boeuf, one from Jay Abraham, and finally the Guerrilla Marketing manual from Jay Conrad Levinson.

Jay Conrad Levinson's book changed everything for me. More on that later.

Here's the strange thing. My life had never been about reading. My life was slitting and watching and observing. That isn't a bad thing but it doesn't give you the details or the fast track.

I read all of these books (apart from Tom Peters - I just couldn't get it) from start to finish. Each bit of new detail felt almost like another part of a puzzle falling into place. True, I could never get everything done that I had read but I did what I could and slowly put small things into place in my salon one piece at a time.

Was my salon any different?

My Needs, My Life & The Difference

This got me thinking more about marketing my salon from a new approach.

Clients had a choice of seven salons in the village where my little salon was. Why would they choose mine? Do they really want to buy a haircut that all of the salons were selling (cut and dry) or do they want to buy a happier life through looking and feeling good?

Looking good might get them the perfect partner. Looking good made them feel sexy, gorgeous, or handsome every morning they faced a mirror. Looking and feeling good increased the way they performed on a daily basis.

Words were starting to make sense on a mental level, not just a written form level.

A woman or a man whose partner had run away now wanted, and really needed, a new partner to see them as sexy and they wanted to feel loved, adored, sexy, special, and wanted once again.

They knew a new look would help with their confidence, their behaviour, the way they walked and they way they held themselves. In the morning they could look in a mirror and see themselves as this new person rather than the old person that was left abandoned.

In other words, hair had become part of her inner resurrection to a new life or becoming a new man or woman once again. Just cool, right! Now you might know this, but at that time I certainly didn't. It changed everything for me.

The client's real-life deeper needs had to be addressed in my words. Just like my needs were addressed through the brilliant Paul Mitchell ads. I wanted a particular lifestyle and that meant a successful business.

She or he wanted a new partner in his or her life and that meant a new sexy, dramatic, cool, and seductive look though a haircut. I could do that!

So rather than my ads and flyer spelling out the name of my salon, address and what my salon did, they now started to take a new shape and approach.

When the Headline is a Thought on Paper

I still had no idea the top bit was called a headline. As far as I was concerned, it was just called the first line, but that first line had to say what the client was thinking.

So, I imagined a woman talking to herself in the morning. I imagined I could see her feeling fed-up, depressed, and sad. I would see her waking up or in the middle of the day. I would see her walking to the mirror in the bathroom with average lighting. I could see her looking into the mirror at the creases around her eyes, her stressed out hollowing skin, and her hair looking a mess. She felt older and past it. And then I would see her thoughts and knew from speaking to clients daily she would be saying to herself.

"When's the last time I changed my hair?"

She was asking herself a question. The question wasn't only related to her hair, it was ultimately related to how she was looking and feeling deeper inside. She understands that a change of look can change everything. You know it can, I know it can.

The new hair requires new make-up, new clothes, new perfume, and new actions. This would in return make her feel good about herself again. Her confidence wouldn't force a partner to her, but would attract the right person into her life.

Her needs were now being fulfilled through a promise that started in the basics of the ad. This is the approach that I ethically stole from the ideas Paul Mitchell advertising had given me and literally transformed my business almost overnight.

Here is something else interesting I learnt. Once the core needs of a client are met, this can affect pricing in a most powerful way.

When I started creating adverts that met the core needs I also took a new direction in pricing in my hair salon. When I had created these new 'needs filling' ads I also decided that this would take a new audience for my highly improved salon services.

This new audience would not only have to pay more but would be very happy to pay more for my hairdressing services that would meet their every need.

I went for a decent price increase but I also had to be strong. Doing this made me feel sick, but I also knew I had no option. My fee for the client on the Saturday evening at closing in those days was £6.95. Two days later when I opened after the weekend my new prices were set at £18.95. That's a massive increase.

What do you think happened?

Clients loved the service because core needs that cannot be explained were being met. Core needs that can never be discovered over conference room tables or fixation marketing meetings or core needs that the average repeating marketer would never even think of were being met.

Once a core need is met the resistance to your sale is as good as dissolved.

Over a two-day period not only had I almost tripled my prices but the result beyond was only to make my salon much busier. This was when I realised that price wasn't the issue to my bigger success.

I didn't have to be the same price as everyone else. I didn't have to do the same as everyone else. I could charge what I liked as long as a true value exchange was being created at the same time.

The price only reflected the return on investment. The investment was more than a haircut it was a feeling of elevation, worthiness, sexiness, and a deeper feeling of just feeling good about self. You cannot buy this kind of stuff, so once a service is found to deliver it the price has now become a long secondary option.

And the cool part ...

I realised that when a price is the same as everyone else's price you are giving the buyer the final decision. I realised that a client would phone many salons and make a choice of salon on a personal decision – not price. How could it be price when all prices, all perceptive looks of the sales were almost identical?

Out of seven small salons in the village where my first salon was located all the salons charged around £6.95, as did I when I opened. Now I was the only salon that was charging £18.95. Price alone made me standout in the most dramatic way and this only increased my salon takings by three times!

I had gone from no confidence in my salon to incredible confidence and the feeling that I can now take on the world from my little salon. After seeing the reaction to the words, I had written in my adverts I started to write out what I felt a client was asking themselves based on what I heard them say to me in the salon. This isn't and wasn't business, it was basic needs being met through a hairdressing service.

I also discovered the following in my salon and the results were huge.

As you may know, in the hair industry it is pretty traditional that a stylist meets the client once the client is sitting in the chair where they have their haircut. Most times the client's hair would even be washed before the stylist meets the client.

But a client will arrive into my salon nervous – this is a predisposition of any client going into any new salon – and then meet the stylist when in fact they will feel at their worst or most vulnerable moment. Wet, flat, unstyled hair, and possibly eye make running after water splashes. Not only are most clients unlikely to open up about anything but also they are unlikely to spend more money than they have to whilst at the salon.

I knew my clients were thinking more than I could know so I wanted to know more about how they were thinking. Once I knew how they were thinking and feeling I could make them an offer to solve their current thoughts and feelings.

Once their thoughts and feelings are solved not only does a client relax, they also develop a trust beyond the usual trust. By the way, the best way to find out what they are thinking is to simply – ask them!

I thought about different ways to find out the problems and came to the conclusion that the way a doctor would find out would be to sit face to face, ask searching questions, and then offer the perfect solution. This was also the way mum had built her mini health food empire so this was a good time to put a lesson into practice.

So I created a questionnaire on a clipboard just like a doctor would have used (iPad now), I would sit face-to-face with my new clients and then after introducing myself would go through the questions one at a time and tick off the answers. I created the sheets with three layers. White on the top, yellow next, and then pink. The client was given a copy of the sheet. This would be an agreement that what was discussed was the clients thoughts and not just the thoughts of a hairdresser.

Once the sheet was filled out after 20-minutes of consulting I would then offer the solution. Now remember this. The client had arrived for a £18.95 haircut. After a consultation like this they understood their hair problems were more than a haircut.

I understood to get the desired results it would take a little more. This would result in a recommendation or advice or myself. For example if the client needed more volume a colour could give her more volume and texture. If she needed her hair to look thicker I would advise the client use certain products on her hair at home, and so on.

Once that was recommended and the service was carried through the client would have another fear and it was this...

"How am I going to manage my hair at home?"

I realised this and would spend extra time showing the client how to manage her hair at home with new products and styling tools. Now here is the thing;

My invoices at the checkout went from £18.95 to as high as £200 on many occasions (this was 1989/90).

This whole process led me into a different hairdressing path. It had no longer become about survival hairdressing but had now become about value exchange hairdressing. I was hungry to be successful and despite the problems early on I also had the drive and energy to overcome anything.

I hadn't sold out. This was still punk rock. I was still breaking the rules. I had become the anti-salon in my area. I was the Johnny Rotten of the local salon trade and the local salons really didn't like what I was doing.

This newly discovered business process got me thinking about something else that I mastered in my second salon. It's worth mentioning now because like everything so far it also applies to your business.

I Discovered The Mind Follows a Path to Buying

I realised that every client goes through a process or path of the mind before a process of buying. It can start at any point and can be started by events of life or just the thirst to change or put things right in their mind through change. When I say change, I of course mean a change of hair.

Going back to the woman or man looking in the mirror, most of the times they don't really notice their hair. Then one day they might see an image and that image is repeated into their mind time and time again. That image is a hairstyle that they don't have but love the idea of having.

They then start to look at their own hair in the mirror and even start to ask others if that hairstyle would suit them. Once other agree (or disagree) the thought process of change has really started.

From the thoughts and initial hair images seen the process is taken to another level by the client. That level involves collecting pictures and ideas for the hairstyle. The images can be collected and once again shown to friends. Eventually the client – let's just say a woman for now – decides to go into a salon and have her hairstyle changed.

At this stage the resistance to paying for a new hairstyle has gone. In their mind they have already paid for and bought the new hairstyle.

Before they get to the salon they go through a salon or stylist search process. They think about their current salon and might reason that they have already been going for three years and no offer of change has been made so the trust isn't there for a redesign.

They then search for a salon and stylist they can trust without risk. This is done through asking friends first, searching online, and looking at ratings online. In my day it was simply a case of asking others.

Once the salon has been decided the client will either make contact with the salon or walk into the salon. They haven't bought into the salon just yet, but they will decide based on reaction they get from the salon staff on the visit.

This can be how the phone call is handled to how the staff reacts as she walks in. At this point a client can still be lost. If lost – cash is lost. I couldn't afford to lose clients like that, could you?

So once I worked out this mental process with clients I then started to test different things on the phone. If a client rang and said I would like to know the price of a restyle in your salon, most salons would then hand over the price list.

Converting Words for the Phone

If they called my salon I had created scripts and rituals that had to be carried out by all of my staff.

Words had now become a critical business building tool in my hairdressing salon. Say the right or the wrong thing meant sink or swim.

Here's an example of the word differences that I had tested time and again.

A local salon on the phone:

'Hi can you tell me the price of a cut and restyle please?'

'Yes from £25.50 up to £45.50'

'OK thank you.'

'OK thank you.'

Then the phone went down.

Any salon I rang at this time had given no thought about the mental word process new clients go through. I still think most salons even today still don't understand this process or give it any real thought.

I had worked out the exact words and I knew the mental journey clients were going through so I picked up the phone this way.

My salon and my carefully worded script:

"Hi can you give me the price of a cut and restyle please?'

'Hi this is Alan speaking. I am happy you called us because we are restyle specialists. This means that when you come into our salon a restyle specialist will sit with you and go through every issue you have with your hair right now, suggest at least six different restyles you can have, give you free advise on how to look after your new restyle, and even show you all the products and tools you will need for your new hairstyle when you get home. Alan is free on Saturday at 2:00 pm shall I book you in then?'

Something magical had taken place and it was this. When the right words are used and the words are triggers (or current thoughts of the client) price was never the issue when the client called. She simply called to break the ice and see if this salon could help her. Also, all of her fears and objections had been covered so she was happy to book in with Alan at 2:30 pm.

Finally, we rarely mentioned the price but we would give an estimate if asked again. The reason is I understood early that price wasn't the issue – value exchange was. This was explained through careful word choice. This was another discovery that was to transform my new salon business.

And as you can see and will understand the journey of any salon client doesn't change and cannot change. The process of buying isn't a process of persuading, it is a process of fulfilment of core needs.

The needs are what persuade the buyer, not the convincing words or the endless barrage of direct attempts to force her to book. Or in lots of cases when I have worked with and tested salon phone answering - as little effort as possible!

Careful words and careful images were my key. The core need was the client wanted to feel safe, feel good, feel sexy, feel wanted, and have a euphoric feeling of her becoming alive after her new look. And believe me, after working in the hairdressing business for over three-decades (since 1982) there is no such thing as six weeks between good and bad hair. Bad hair can destroy a woman's life for way longer than six weeks. So the process of choice is detailed and as precise as it can be.

Marketing Takes Huge Constant Effort

Getting clients through the door takes effort, and constant effort at that. It also takes an ongoing plan of action. A one-off hit was never going to make anything happen.

I learned that waiting for a client to walk through the door was a fool's game. Yes, clients will walk through the door, but it was always faster if I did everything in my power to pull them into my salon much faster rather than sitting and waiting for them to arrive.

Ultimately, with my first salon I realised that I am the one responsible for my salon business being a success or being a failure. There are always things I could do but I had to learn to take action to make my salon business work and happen as fast as possible.

Everything was always a choice but I had to learn how to make the right choices and then take action to make sure of those choices. So now I had started pulling clients in, I wanted to increase the momentum. I now also wanted and needed to be a bigger salon.

I had done this from ground zero and loved it.

I had created two main tag lines.

One was, 'It's the difference that makes us different' The second and the one I settled with was, 'having fun, doing hair, being number one.'

I felt the choice of each word described the salon perfectly. Yes we were having fun when doing hair. aAnd Yes I now had a belief that we were the number one salon.

And we were.

More writing words that work.

More marketing.

More copy.

It was relentless.

The Bigger Salon the Bigger Problems

Around one year into my first salon it was now clear that the premises were far too small. I literally had clients falling out of the front door. On weekends I had even put two benches outside the salon for waiting clients to sit on as we worked through a relentless torrent of clients from 8am to 5:30pm with no stops or breaks. It was insane!

At this stage I was using just one or two flyers that I had created and a regular slot on the local weekly newspaper. Being a village environment, it felt easier to build up a base of clients very quickly.

This is where I realised that loyalty to one salon, although spoken about and thought about as a gospel, didn't really exist. Clients, despite going to one salon for say, ten years or more, would happily, if not nervously, swap salons as long as the feedback from others was good.

I had taken no real notice of the power of referrals or clients coming back for more. I simply arrived at the shop, opened the doors, and worked like a happy slave from morning until night.

And by the way ... I was making a serious attempt at doing things as differently as I could. I played punk music very loud, looked the part, did a lot of crazy stuff in the salon, and felt like I was creating an environment that once visited the clients wouldn't forget. It was working and working like crazy.

Getting Deeper into Marketing & Writing

I'd cut my teeth in my own hair salon business as far as creating ads goes. Although I had to create everything from scratch and create what was needed from flyers to vouchers, my biggest winners were always direct mail.

From as early as 1992 direct mail was the number one way for me to take my business into my marketplace. I never mailed blind and always mailed my existing salon databases.

This wasn't that easy for a couple of reasons. First, computers in small businesses like mine just didn't really exist. All of my client's records were on paper cards. The letters had to be printed at the actual printers unlike how we can very easily do them in our homes or offices today. When computers arrived it was a slow and very laborious job but a job that still had me mailing a minimum of 500+ direct mail pieces every single Tuesday for well over a decade.

When I really got heavily into direct mail in the salon I started using a dot-matrix printer in the salon itself. It could take days to print off 500 letters. The paper also had to be torn from the side perforations and the main sheets also came in one long roll but had perforations. If you don't know the paper was almost like on one endless toilet roll. The noise from the printing was like a small machine gun in the salon!

But I did it because this was business building and it had to be done.

Mastery over direct mail completely exploded my salon business and frankly, I would mail for any reason if I thought it would increase my business – and it did.

Reminders, birthdays, anniversaries, sales, new staff, new products, missing clients, and more, I just never stopped. Each theme for each campaign needed its own copy. I wrote the copy. When I did stop mailing guess what happened? Business slowed. There were times now and then when I would fall out of the habit due to being busy and maybe not mail for a month. Rare, but it did happen. The effect on the salon left gaping holes in the appointment book. Eventually I simply made it a fixed rule that the mailings were printed and stamped on Monday and Tuesday. Then they went out into homes as always.

My letters always had a headline relevant to the reason for sending.

For example, my reminder letters had one headline I never changed. It was this.

'Do you realise its now just over 5-weeks since your last haircut? That means your hair is half an inch longer'

Birthdays were a simple one also…

'Happy birthday Susan, have a wonderful day'

And the letter I would send to missing clients would say,

'Missing. I noticed you are missing from our salon and we'd love you to come back'

This stuff sounds so basic as I write it here, but the letters worked and worked like crazy. Our missing campaigns always pulled an incredible 65% back into the salon and that was a ton of cash. Not bad when an average direct mail is around 0.5%!

And of course I had to write them despite the fact I had no idea or had never been trained to write copy by anyone. I just did it on an intuitive thought of what are the clients think and want.

My biggest responding campaign was always

A letter that said…

When's The Last Time You Changed Your Hair,? as a headline at the top of the letter.

The letter then went into a short explanation of how we were the only and best redesign specialists for hair.

It gave a short story and a few bullets of why we specialise and then a simple call to action. This was the one letter and ad that I ran forever.

But honestly, there was never a format at all. I simply saw good ads and felt if they worked on me when I read them and knew like in my old punk days that I should copy them.

69

The salon was buzzing!

The Car Park and The Big Wall

My salon faced onto a car park. That car park had over 400 spaces. I used to sit looking over that car park from my office window.

One day I had a moment when I noticed that almost everyone walking from their car had to walk down a dark alley at the side of my salon and then onto the main street.

I realised that they all looked up and spent around 30-seconds walking from their car to the street.

No one advertised anything at the back of the shops in those days. It was a bit of a dump and we all parked our cars next to large rubbish bins.

I decided if they are looking up I should put something there. These are the days when signs never came in vinyl they had to be hand-painted.

I called the sign writer and asked him to paint me a sign that would be around 14 ft by 14 ft. It was huge for the type of shop I had.

I don't have a photo of the sign but it said …

High Quality Hairdressing.

Leigh's Only Hair Redesign Specialists.

The wording designed to feed short attention and deliver a perception message. Each word I chose very carefully.

By saying, 'High Quality Hairdressing' what I am really saying is no one else is as good as us. We are the first choice if you want the best.

The town was called Leigh. I was saying if you want a restyle we are the only ones. We weren't of course but no one else said it so I decided to say it. Once I said it no one would say it because they would feel like they are copying.

And by saying, 'Hair Redesign Specialists' I was creating a position that we are the only salon out of 35 that doing redesign. I realised the more I told the more the public accepted what I was telling them.

This huge sign got noticed and again I was getting asked who had been creating my signage. The public and other local businesses noticed what I was doing.

And then there were the windows. The principle was the same and that was I had seconds to share a strong message with them so I covered all of my rear windows with single word posters. I also put thousands of flyers on every car daily until I got fined from the local council.

Please don't forget this was 1991-ish. No one was doing anything remotely like this in the world of hairdressing.

I also decided to copy big city shop windows. All the salons had windows you couldn't see through and if you could it would just be to the waiting area from the window. I decided to make social statements in my large windows. I would then tie those statements into what we were doing in the salon.

I would use two words on huge sheets like;

Cruelty Free

Zero Testing

Save Planet Earth

And more. Again the principle of using as few words as possible to make as big a statement as possible worked.

The public loved it and believe me even the local press were taking notice.

The power and effect of using words on my little salon business were just huge and I was getting the hang of this writing thing. Again it was all very intuitive for me yet it was doing what I wanted it to do. Honestly … I wanted to make money and be number one.

Not only was it working like crazy for me, but the town's original number one salon, who I felt threatened by most of the time because they really were a great salon.

One day I had a call from the owner. I loved his work but he never seemed to like me. He asked if I could visit him at the end of the day on a coming Saturday. I replied I would.

When I went his salon was beautiful. It had been fitted amazingly well. He also had a school above his salon that a large amount of cash had been spent on.

I was curious as to why he wanted me to go. I went and he was in tears. He offered me his salon to buy. I refused and they closed after over 30-years. A real shame but he always told me he was an artist and wouldn't advertise. I advertised and I mastered words and it showed.

I had gone from a new start-up hairdressing salon to the town's number one salon in just 18-months. I will say this; my marketing was brutally relentless.

But I never did discounts. At the time I wasn't sure why but it felt like a hole I would get back out from.

What a real shame to lose a business after 30-years because you felt ads were a bad route to take.

I had learned some incredible stuff and that stuff had changed everything.

The Little I Knew About Copy Was This

Here is what I knew and learned about writing copy over those years. It's a principle that stands as I write to you now.

It either works, or it doesn't work.

It had to work, failure could never be my choice. I didn't know anything about formulas as such I just wrote the ads and used them like crazy.

I had a young family, I had a home to be paid for, and I had other expenses and luxuries I wanted in my life. If the ads failed nothing happened in life. If they worked I got my rewards.

I suppose that, for me, is my own personal purpose for copywriting. Yet, there is another secret that I will share with you because I know If you are reading this you are probably looking and searching for some holy grail of copywriting.

Here is mine and it has never failed me once – never.

I knew the clients or customers are always having an internal conversation with themselves. That conversation might be about colour, restyle, how bad they looked, or simply a change of hairdresser.

I would sit and think about what the clients were saying in the salon or what I thought and knew they were already saying in their heads. This was the conversation.

They are already tuned-in and just waiting for someone to strike up or open the conversation.

For example my friend loves to talk about the wonders of space. He bores most people when he talks about it because they get totally lost in his one-sided conversation. Eventually he realises and stops talking. The conversation is in his head, but he only reacts when another person starts that same conversation.

When anyone shows an interest in his conversation he comes to life and reacts and responds in a way that only that conversation can make him react.

I found hair was the same. It was never about any kind of persuasion for me, it was always about joining the conversation.

The interesting thing of me over those years was most of the other salons we had feedback from felt our marketing was cheap, cheesy, amateurish, and tacky. Maybe it was from a cosmetic point, but all I knew was this;

The salon was packed from morning until night. We charged the highest prices and had stylists clambering to work in our salon. We had snatched the number one position from under the noses of all of the other top salons in just 18-months. That was obvious to anyone who passed my incredibly busy salon.

My ads were everywhere. They could be seen in markets, florist, clothes shops, food halls, on buses, on billboards, on the radio, in newspapers. I mean everywhere. I even had flyers put into kids school bags targeting mums.

I was writing ads, letters, vouchers, offers, and flyers almost everyday. Once I had what worked I simply ran and ran them until they stopped working.

My teeth had been cut as a copywriter or marketing man but even at this stage I had never read or seen or heard of the word 'copywriter.'

I do want to finish this part saying this to you. During this period was a time in my life when I really didn't have the time to endlessly read or take courses. Taking action and pushing forward was the only thing I had time for. I would only read to find out a single detail - never a full book.

My external influence was almost microscopic on my copy and in fact the only real influences was how I would observe successful businesses and try and copy something from them in my own little way (and Paul Mitchell.)

I only owned one truly influential book (my business Bible at the time) that I accidentally picked up in London called Guerrilla Marketing by Jay Conrad Levinson.

I still have my yellow paged, well used, ripped, scribbled on and coffee stained original print version signed by Jay himself. If it weren't for Jay and his influence I doubt my salon would have been built as fast.

Later in 2008 I was to accidentally meet Jay face to face. We became good friends from that day forward. I will explain this interesting and almost inevitable story in greater detail for you later.

Whats next?

From Hairdresser to Writer to Whatever

Let me finish the hairdressing bit on this.

I owned three hairdressing salons for 17-years. They were the number one salons in that area. They never really saw slow days.

My turnover went from around £30,000 in year one to £300,000 in the last year for my big salon. I'd call that a result for sure.

For me everyday was marketing day. It was never a single event, it was part of my own daily processes. For me it was as important as cleaning the toilet or making sure we had coffee for clients.

I now had hundreds of flyers, posters, signs, letters, vouchers, handouts, referrals, hand notes, mirror signs, and more everywhere. I used signage on transport, buses, cinema, outdoor boards. You name it, I was doing it.

I could spend hours thinking over single words to choose. Every word had to be a word that had been carefully chosen from what I thought clients were thinking. I even asked what they were thinking.

Nothing was accidental apart from later being named a copywriter.

This took time, patience, learning, but most important - doing, lots of just getting it down and doing it.

I still hadn't become this copywriter thing yet I had, I just didn't know it. I was writing stuff almost everyday for my salons. Practice was the key, but for me it wasn't practice for practice sakes, it was just something I had to do for my salon's success.

Then a ton of weird things started to happen in the salon.

Crazy Colin, "Who Writes Your Ads?"

This guy was nuts!

I used to have a crazy client named Colin (name changed). He was genuinely lovable and genuinely nuts. For him everything in life was an opportunity. His highly charged and highly positive approach to life was alien to me at the time, but he was always ramped with energy for the next big thing.

One day Colin walked into my salon as per usual. He loved women and women loved him. He would make his big presence known by shouting to all the girls in the salon of his arrival. They mostly ignored him, they thought he was crazy.

One day as I began to cut his hair he asked me,

"Alan, who writes those ads you run in the newspapers?"

I replied

"I do."

He laughed and said,

"You're just a hairdresser, c'mon who writes them as I have a new computer company that I want to push out and I love your ads and letters."

I explained to him once more I wrote them. When he was finally convinced he asked me if I would write some ads for him. I told him of course.

His new company was a computer company. He was buying components from China and had guys putting all the parts together here in the U.K. in the garage at his home. These were called personal computers (later know as the PC)and he would sell them into people's homes. This was the early-to-mid-nineties.

The problem here was not many people had computers at this time and I would say most didn't really see the need for them. Dial up was terrible, as was Windows and the install of AOL portals discs to get online.

Anyway, blindly I wrote the ads and he ran them in the newspapers right away. Incredibly, the guy began selling computers like there was no tomorrow. The ads were basic but we seemed to have hit a conversation about the future.

I never got paid, but I was given two computers for writing the ads. One Pentium 90 for home and one for my office. The one at home got used now and then, but there really wasn't a great deal I could do with it. The one in the office lay there collecting dust because I just didn't have time to learn how to use it. I was still writing my ads by hand and running to the printers.

This was one of my first transition points into writing ads for another person or business other than myself. It was also the first of many times my ads began to get noticed. I never gave another thought to writing ads for anyone else; I felt like I was simply doing a favour for my client.

Then this happened.

The Accountant's Letter – More Huge Sales

Not too long after that another guy named Tim came into the salon. He asked me about the direct mail his wife and himself had been getting from my salon on a regular basis.

He was an accountant and wanted letters to send out to his customers. He wanted to push his new accounting software program, which again, he was a very early adopter. The conversation came around to who does them, etc. Again I explained I do it all myself. He then asked if I could advise, consult and help him create a series of letters like the ones I was mailing, but for his software.

I said I would and asked him to leave it with me. The salon was so busy, how would I get time to do these letters for him? Anyway, when I had an hour or so I ran upstairs into my tiny office and typed away on my new Pentium 90 a series of three letters he could use for direct mail. I copied the three-mailer system I used for reminding my clients.

Letter one was a standard offer. Letter two had an increased offer for those who didn't respond, and letter three had an offer designed to get them onboard at a reasonable acquisition cost.

The letters were completed for him. I'd spent just one hour writing them. I called him to explain he could come and pick them up on a floppy disc or I could mail them to him (emailing them in those days was a total impossibility).

A couple of days later he arrived to pick up the floppy disc. Payment was never discussed, but he handed me an envelope and simply said I hope this is enough for doing these. I took the envelope and put it on my desk.

We talked some more and then he left. I had to rush downstairs to do a haircut or two. I actually forgot about the envelope because I was just busy. A couple of days later he called me and said he loved the letters but the grammar was terrible. He mentioned nouns and verbs and commas and more. I simply replied that it would be fixed and checked and that I would fix that no worries.

To be honest, I had no idea what he was talking about. I always wrote my own stuff and simply sent it, typos and all. It isn't that I avoided doing the grammar I just had no idea about grammar. In fact, I only starting to learn that stuff around early 2000 when I fully transitioned into writing for a living. My ads for myself always worked so it was never something I gave much thought to unless someone mentioned it.

I had to be a little humble and find a neighbour who was actually my old school teacher (the same one I mentioned who advised me to write the flyer) to explain to me what grammar was and the changes that were needed. Once the changes were done the client sent out his new letters. Around six weeks later when he returned for his haircut he was so happy about the results from his letters that he had sold thousands upon thousands of products from them.

Just amazing! I was amazed.

By the way, I finally opened the envelope that had been lying on my desk. It contained £1,500 for the one hour of writing I had done for my client. At that same time, I was earning around £350 **per week** running my three salons 24/7!

That got me thinking, but I still hadn't given anything thought to any changes of career or even writing ads or consulting with clients for a living. I was Alan the hairdresser and that felt like I was Alan the hairdresser!

Then this happened.

The 47% Sales Letter

I had a sales rep named John (name changed). He had decided to start his own company and had invested a ton of investor's cash into the company. The amount was around £1.5 million.

One day he came into the salon and told me of his woes whilst upstairs in my office. He loved the letters and marketing I was sending out as I was the only salon he knew of doing such intensive marketing like I was doing. He asked me about how I was doing it and also explained that he was on his last throw of the dice for his own company. He wanted help so I offered.

He had been trying direct mail for months with terrible results. He would mail 5000 prospects and tell them how amazing the new products were. He would mention a meeting place with a time and date where they could come along and see the new products. He was lucky to get 2-3 responses from 5000. His wife had also told him that if this carried on she would leave him (after he sold her car to pay for yet another campaign).

"Alan can you help me?"

I told him to leave it with me as I was also a very busy hairdresser. I thought about this problem and offered a solution. It was this.

Create a simple three series of mailers (yep). Send to just 100 of his best prospects. Make an offer so irresistible that on the open night he would make no money – it would cost him money – but over the coming year it would be worth a small fortune to him and his company. This would convert the interested into clients.

He thought is sounded ridiculous, after all, how can 100 prospects be a better chance than 5000? Easy, and I knew exactly how because I had been doing this for a few years in my own salon. It wasn't uncommon for me to send maybe ten mailers to a very targeted group with great results. So the letters were crafted and he mailed them out.

My phone rang.

"Alan is that you, it's John?"

"Yes, what's up?"

"I have 47 salon owners booked into our presentations from the letters. I just can't believe it"

I did believe it because I'd been hammering out mailers for years at this stage.

On the night, all 47 salons arrived and all 47 salons signed up. Not only did he have a 47% response rate to the campaign, but also, he had orders from these guys over the coming year of just over £800,000!

The question is how? The answer is the same. I had to produce results like I have always had to produce results.

I got inside the head of the salon owners and gave them what they were already thinking about. Solved problems and offered them more ways into strong profits. That's all they wanted. This solved it.

By the way, I never got paid a penny for this but this is a story so strong it was worth doing so I can share it with you and share it with others. It was also worth doing to learn the massive power of laser target marketing.

The momentum into change had started to build, I just didn't realise it.

The Car Sales King With Half a Brain – Literally!

One day in the salon I was sitting in my office opening my morning pile of letters. It was from a local car sales garage named Kings. They sold used or import German sports cars as their specialisation. The letter was to sell me their latest truck. The truck was perfect for a small-town builder or delivery guy. But I was a hairdresser so why were they sending me this letter?

I would drive past this garage everyday on the way to my salon. I was already interested in the garage because they had the only new shape VW Beetle in the UK that I had seen. I was currently driving a 1976 restored VW 1303S Super Beetle in Summer of Love orange that I loved. I also loved the idea of buying a new shape VW beetle.

One day I decided to drive into the garage on the way back from the salon. As I pulled in the obvious brightness of my classic bright orange Beetle and the noise that went from the back of the car pulled all of the staff out onto the forecourt.

The owner of the place then came out and told me how his father had one of the very first VW franchises in a town named Wigan in the north of England. He loved my car. He then asked how I knew about the garage. I told him I had a letter for a new builder's truck. He asked if I wanted a truck. I told him no because I am a hairdresser that has a salon.

So, I asked him this.

"Why are you sending a hairdresser a letter for a truck?"

He then went onto tell me the database was just too complex to sort out so they sent letters to everyone and especially local businesses. No kidding, they had one room packed with handwritten cards with data on from their decades in business.

I told him I write a lot of direct mail and would be happy to help him for an incredible deal on a new VW Beetle.

He then told me he was importing around twenty new Audi TT sports cars and he wanted to sell them as fast as possible. Usually it could take around a year to shift them. Any of the cars not sold would have to be moved on at a loss.

So, I stripped back some data for them until we found people that had bought a sports car from them around three years earlier. I crafted a short series of three letters (see the tried, tested and used pattern here) with an offer the readers hopefully just couldn't refuse.

He then sent out the letters. In just three weeks (21-days) those letters sold 18 new Audi cars. They had never seen anything like it. As a thank you they gave me £5,000 worth of extra built into the new VW Beetle I bought from them.

They thought it was magic. It was. It wasn't. I was just repeating what I had been doing in my hairdressing salons for years. Tapping into the client's internal conversation and offering what they are already looking for.

Honestly it wasn't hard. It always feels like pure common sense to me. It was never over thinking but just a pure conversational and simple message.

Here is what you are thinking about. Here is what we can make sure you have what you're thinking about. Here it is a price you'll kill for. It's a no brainer, but to sell 18 high-end cars from a single mailer was pretty awesome to say the least! And I got my new VW at a knock down price with over £5,000 of extras added. Their sales were well over a million. This is the first time I had written a campaign that had generated such massive sales.

We became friends for years after this. One thing worth mentioning is that one of the owners had half a brain and I mean literally half a brain. One full side of his brain had been removed to prevent a problem that he had experienced since being a child. He was eccentric but functioned absolutely as any other normal person. It just shows the magnificence of the human body. And of course the magnificence of direct response marketing when kept stripped back and simple.

If it is kept stripped back I am not saying the outcome can be scientifically determined, it can't, but the chance of a success are increased dramatically. I was still a hairdresser and I was still just playing around.

Then I got another phone call.

Dave The Accountant & the Orange Beetle

One day I was in my salon when my phone rang.

"Is Alan the adman there please"

"Hello, this is Alan"

"orange beetle, are you the guy that drives that old orange beetle?"

"Yes" I laughed.

"My name is Dave, I was told to ring you."

So, we talked. He wanted to create a system that he could run and run to sell his financial and accounting services. We arranged to meet. I had to arrange the meeting in between hairdressing clients.

Finally, I had some time and drove over to his huge offices in Cheshire, England. As I drove into the car park between the two-huge red brick pillars the noise from my old vw orange beetle bounced from every wall, shook every window and pulled every person in that building to a window to see what the hell the noise was or into the car park itself.

I parked my old beetle between the new Jaguar car and the very big and very black and very shiny Rolls Royce.

"orange beetle," a voice shouted from the upstairs fire escape. It was Dave. He smiled and we finally met.

Guess what we did? I once again created a 3-step letter program for him that he could use as long as he wanted to use it for. He loved it, it worked, and he managed to upsell literally tens of thousands of services. I got paid and this was the first of many jobs we did together.

Changes like this were coming thick and fast.

The Calls Kept on Coming

Then a window company called me for ads. Then a jeweller called me from Mississippi of all places. Then a bread shop called me and then a tree surgeon from Texas called me. The list went on. I have no idea how I was getting such a reputation, but common sense told me this;

Do great work and those who are searching for a great marketing man that can write great copy will change everything. It was changing everything and maybe faster than I was expecting.

At this stage I had done no marketing or pushing of this new business because as far as I was concerned it wasn't really a business. I was still a hairdresser and a salon owner and that was that.

This was just a favour here and there I was doing for people who asked. The only real problem I started to have was the volume of people who were now asking.

I had no website because they really didn't exist in the mainstream then, or even a card. I didn't really see it as a serious business despite the fact I was getting paid large amounts for what felt like something I could do with my eyes shut.

It's easy to forget at this point I had been writing sales copy since 1985. I had made every mistake possible and discovered the power of conversational and direct writing.

I understood how one word could have more power than twenty words.

I understood how asking questions in my letters and ads increased the response rates.

I now understood that telling the reader exactly what they had to do really helped them to respond.

I also knew that the more pressure I added to the client in the copy the less they would buy.

So many small things were huge in this new world, but I had spent at least ten years doing this stuff every day for my own salon business and the results were as clear as day.

Then I came across this.

The Copywriters Board Online

The money I was getting paid for a few words here and there was insane, but I was loving it! I had begun to seriously consider selling my 20-year old hairdressing business. My family thought I had gone totally crazy.

I still knew little-to-nothing about the copywriting world until, one day I found a website called The Copywriters Board. This was a forum hosted and owned by copywriter Michel Fortin. Today Michel is absolutely one of my best friends, but at that time, I didn't know him.

Anyway, I joined the board and discovered this whole breed of writers that talked endlessly about copywriting and their expertise.

It was alien for me to talk so much about myself. I am a doer and needed to make things happen not talk about things that might happen. I noticed right away that a lot of the guys on these boards simply wanted to be 'right' and prove another writer wrong. I didn't care, I didn't have time to care. All I knew was, that when I write for myself or for a client it worked or it didn't work.

I understood branding and positioning and standing out in a busy marketplace. I had been doing this for my salons for well over a decade. I understood the importance of positioning my salon, so the same would apply here for my consultancy business. I understood that the only way to be seen was to get seen. After all I was marketing my salons every single day to make sure they stayed busy, and I was never to be forgotten by the public. It worked in my hairdressing business so I knew it would work here.

From what I was seeing most copywriters had copywriting sites like johthecopywriter.com. They had the word 'copywriter' in there. I didn't want that as I didn't really consider myself a copywriter. I was just a businessman that seemed to find the right way forward with good ideas that solved problems.

I did learn a lot from the copywriters board. It really did open a new way of doing things I had never heard of before. It wasn't really the way an old punk was going to do things. I didn't need opinions, I just wanted to see what was happening in this strange new world.

I met some incredible guys on that board, but I would say a lot of the copywriters there felt stiff, rigid and endlessly in competition with each other (I'm better than you). Too many fixations on any kind of rule wasn't going to work for me

I had been doing this writing thing for a long time before then, and I knew how adaptable I had to be when it comes to creating great ads and results. The formulas I read about on that board were a long distance away from what I had been doing for my own writing clients and myself.

Time for me to leave. The orange beetle was about to arrive.

FF3300 the Orange Beetle

Actually, there is a short story behind this.

As I mentioned earlier, I had this beautiful 1976 summer of love 1303s super beetle that I had restored. I drove this car everywhere. The noise was deafening, but once seen and heard you didn't quickly forget him.

I would go and see every client in this car rather than the BMW I also had. I knew it would always make a strong impression. I understood from my salon business the huge importance of standing out. My salon was in a town of 35 salons. The only way we could be number one was to do the opposite of everyone else and that is what I did by using this car.

I wanted to do the same with my consulting and copy business.

I would estimate that almost every call I got said exactly the same.

"Is that the guy with the orange beetle?"

The impact was so huge, I couldn't ignore it.

A little known fact was before then I had tried setting up a website with a weird name in the late-mid-90s. I can't quite remember what is was called, but it was something like … The Bigger Forrest …

Forrest after my name of course. Who on earth is going to remember that?

So, I ran with the brand name of Orange Beetle Ltd. I branded everything around the name and played heavily on the colour in every aspect of this new business.

My colour palette was the same colour used for the cover of this book.

HEX: FF3300

Why so specific? I also knew the power of a colour or a meme. I wanted to be able to build the association with a single colour (my salons had a specific blue and a particular font I never deviated from).

Is is true that a colour can carry so much power?

How about this colour … HEX: FF3b5998?

It's probably one of the most recognised colours on the planet for a business.

Facebook blue.

Check this out.

Once I was walking along the main street in Sydney, Australia, where I had been invited to lecture. As I walked down the street I heard a voice shout …

"Orange is that you? Hey orange g'day mate."

I looked over the street and a guy came rushing over the street to me.

"Is it you? Alan from orange beetle? What are you doing all the way over here?"

This happened and has happened on many occasions to me. You cannot underestimate the power of a colour in a brand. I love brands and love branding all of my businesses.

It's a strangely interesting thing for me to observe so many modern copywriters say and write things against branding. Strange because the massive power of a brand can be so huge, it's immeasurable.

For me and my three-decades plus experience that is rejection of branding is stupid and uninformed business practice. This is usually related from what someone else has said rather than real-life experience.

I began to build.

Let My New Brand Be Built

I probably need a website. Probably a business card. Maybe not. Whatever!

So, I jumped online and ordered my chosen domain name. I couldn't get OrangeBeetle.com only OrangeBeetle.co.uk.

With all of my domains I learnt very quickly .com is always the best option. For me it sounds bigger (a bit like Blank Face Presents) and feels like a stronger position to be in, almost like the only option. I wanted orangebeetle.com but a software company had taken it, so I registered.co.uk instead.

But just in case I put a back-order on the .com version of the domain. Then totally unexpectedly, maybe a year later I received an email that told me am now the owner of OrangeBeetle.com. The software company had forgotten to renew, so I was now the new owner. They asked for it back, I refused!

Karma came back to kick my ass later. In 2007 I forgot to renew a main domain name of hairee.com. A German guy picked up my domain right away and refused to give it back unless I paid him £10,000. Screw him. I bought a new domain and put the website there at salonpunk.com

I can laugh now but it wasn't funny then. Not only was my ex-wife out to kill me I had lost an income source through stupidity.

Don't play with karma. Karma loves to payback.

Anway, Orangebeetle.com was now here and I decided to build a proper business with it. This was from 1999.

I now had two real orange beetles. My beloved 1976 classic 1303S super beetle and a new model I had custom painted from green to the same classic 1976 colour.

I made sure everything associated with orange beetle was the same over the top ff3300 orange. I even bought an orange kilt (Scottish dress) that I would wear on stage when I was speaking or to important events.

I knew this; just like my salon had to stand out, the same was for orange beetle. I had to be remembered and create mass coverage to be seen. This was critical. I had to create a big reputation for brilliant work and get the attention of the right people as fast possible.

Direct marketing, consulting, and strategic business building and then … a little of the copywriting stuff was added. I was still never that sure about the copywriter thing. As far as I was concerned copywriting (or words) was part of a machine. The machine had to include the outcome, the pathway, the strategy, the tactics, the angle and approach and so on. Copy or words were simply a part of that, so I offered writing copy as an add-on service.

(the truth is in those days I really didn't know what I was as a business. It felt like I was just helping people and they were willing to pay me for it).

In the early days, online it was easy to get a page one position online in Yahoo, Northern Light,Night Owl or AltaVista and all of the other search engines and directories. Google hadn't been born. This gave me another new but thrilling problem. I began getting clients from all over the globe asking for my skilled services.

No big deal today, but you have to remember for a village lad this was a huge deal. I wasn't well travelled or informed yet here I was trying to satisfy clients in Mississippi, Sydney or even places like Singapore.

Orange beetle was exploding and exploding fast. Time to do this.

It's Time Too Seriously Rethink My Career

Another small problem, but confusing problem; my salon had started getting calls like "Can I speak to Alan with the orange beetle." No-one had a clue what was going on. The staff would reply there is no one here that does that, we are a hairdressing salon. I didn't tell my staff my new business for a long while just in case it made them nervous for their jobs.

One day a guy named Neil Stafford walked into the salon. I was cutting hair at the time. He asked the girl on reception if he had the address correct. He said he was looking for a marketing company called orange beetle? She hadn't a clue. He said the address on the website for Orange Beetle Direct Marketing is the same as here at this address? She still had no idea.

The receptionist told him it must be a mistake. He said it can't be. The receptionist asked what is the persons name you are looking for. He replied 'Alan.' They told him the only Alan here is a hairdresser.

I then heard my name and walked over. I told him I was Alan. He said, "you look like a hairdresser doing a haircut." I replied, "I am," and smiled at him. He looked very confused. The girls had no idea what was going on. I explained to him that I am Alan from Orange Beetle. He was still confused. I asked him to wait in reception with my salon clients and when I had finished cutting hair we went upstairs to my office. In the office I explained everything. We both laughed.

My staff stood watching and listening to what on earth was going on. It felt like the time had come to make the full shift into a new career.

Neil - the new client was confused, but he became an orange beetle client.

I created his first ever 11% response direct mailer that pulled a huge 11% response. We are still fiends to this day.

Neil, it's your turn to pay for lunch!

The Full Transition Into Copy Consultancy

It's now around the year 2000.

I have orangebeetle.com and I have this idea about taking this consultancy thing forward. I tell my first wife. She freaks out. Everyone in my life thinks I am going crazy to sell my salons. I probably am. They'd built me a massive house and given me a very good life despite the endless hours and staffing problems. Still, I've had enough and want out of the salon business.

Although I am self-employed not only are my wages a fraction of what OrangeBeetle.com had started to pay me. I was also sick of the long hours my 7-day weeks and the managing of a large teams. It really was time for life change. By the way my life does seem to hit change every 15-years and it had passed that point.

Truthfully, I didn't feel that confident about writing and promising results for others despite the track record for my own business and the few other clients I had attracted.

I would say I was feeling a little scared of dealing with clients for this reason. I was scared of the fact that I wasn't sure if they would get the results. Yes, I'd had them in a small amount for my clients and huge amounts in my salons, but it still made me feel a little uneasy.

Also in the hairdressing game clients were handing over £50-100. In my consultancy business clients were handing over tens of thousands of pounds.

I knew nothing about this as a business. All I knew was what I had been doing in my salons. I knew hairdressing inside out. I was a respected stylist who's clients would even fly in for a haircut. My style was noticeable and remember.

Yet the new industry I knew zero about..

One day a client called me. I clearly remember I was walking my dog around a lake at the time. He first told me how much he loved the letters and the system I had explained to him. After the praise he then said;

"Just one thing you will be doing the grammar and punctation right? There are commas and apostrophes and other bits missing or wrong."

I quickly responded, "Yes, of course that will be perfect when delivered." I had no idea what he was talking about.

This had started to happen on more than one occasion. The reality was grammar is something I had no idea about. At this point I still didn't know what an apostrophes was or how one should be used. Let's be honest you don't need to know that stuff when you're cutting hair. I mean no one ever said to me I want my hair like this and please add an apostrophe!

I knew nothing about this as a business. All I knew was what I had been doing in my salons. I knew hairdressing inside out. I was a respected stylist who's clients would even fly in for a haircut. My style was noticeable and remembered by clients.

Yet this new industry of writing copy I knew zero about.It was an alien environment for me.

I had never dealt with this type of customer. I had never done a consultation for a B2B client.

I just had no idea. And then there were the other technicalities of this industry.

I mentioned my abhorrence to spelling and grammar earlier. It's just something I really never felt the need to learn, yet I understand I need to know and at least make an effort to understand the basics.

And to be truthful this was a whole new uncomfortable experience for me. I was totally out of my comfort zone at every level but I felt determined to learn on the go and keep pushing forward.

So, I made a decision before I went full-time in direct marketing.

This is what I did.

I Went Back To School

I would have to reeducate myself if I wanted to deliver my very best. How? I wasn't a reader, but I was good at getting a feel for things that worked and modelled them well until I could shape them into what I wanted. Yet I still need to be educated just like I need to be trained to be a good at my hairdressing skills.

To be a great hairdresser I had to practice daily. When I started hairdressing I was still a gardener so I had to find time to learn. I would have to do a learning process like this if I wanted to progress fast.

I know I wasn't starting from ground zero because as I'd already mentioned I had been creating and writing for my salons for years at this point.

I also wondered where would I get time in a crazy busy life to do this? My average days consisted of the following.

I had three salons to run. I had to leave the house at 7:30 am daily. I had many staff to manage. I had to write adverts and do haircuts and manage my salon businesses. The day was very full. I was also building a large house myself. I had to do this when I got home in the evenings. I could very easily do that building project into 2am.

Also during this time I was a practicing fundamentalist Christian minister. This meant five meetings a week and a ministry.

As you can see, the whole idea of stealing time to educate myself was never going to be easy. It wasn't.

I also had four very young kids and was in the middle of building my own huge house and living in a caravan or mobile home in a field surrounded by sheep.

When I got home in the evening from my salons I would eat, play with my kids and then carry on working on my house until well after midnight. Time wasn't on my side.

But I committed to making it happen and made a start. I didn't over think how things would happen. As far as I was concerned just thinking and reading wasn't going to get me anywhere. I had to do it so that is what I did. So I started doing and doing like crazy!

I needed to be guided by the very best.

David Ogilvy

This man changed my life.

I discovered and bought two books. One was a book by a guy named David Ogilvy. His book was called Ogilvy on Advertising. If you read and follow one book in your copy career almost everything you need to know is in this single book. Ogilvy was my dead mentor. I will throw this in here.

The information in this £10 book has made me hundreds upon hundreds of thousands of pounds since late 90s and that is no exaggeration.

I loved it, devoured it, copied from it, referred to it and read again and again and again until it felt like I could produce words like David Ogilvy. I also tried to find out as much as I could about the actual man. I believe that once you can get inside the head of the person you can understand more about how the person thinks. I did this with David Ogilvy.

Like I said earlier I also needed to try and understand some technical aspects of writing and creating strategic work for clients. I also discovered and bought a large book by Herschel Gordon Lewis on copywriting. I found it incredibly hard to read and follow, but I stuck with it until I felt like I had a good framework of understanding.

This helped me to write and manage my copy, but also understand some of the technical aspects behind words and grammar.

I also had a long history of sales letters from the salon, but never had any training to write them. Looking at them today they were packed with typos - every one of them.

Herschel Gordon Lewis also had an incredible gem of a book called, 'Sales Letters That Sizzle.' Probably the best book on the subject any copywriter can own. I devoured every line of that book. That book generated for me hundreds of resounds of pounds over the years.

For my reading and education this was about it (maybe one or two others as time went forward but not many.) Apart from that I practiced and wrote something every single day (I still do.)

And time?

When my kids and family were all asleep I happily studied into the small hours for months after months after months.

I was still writing my own ads for my hairdressing salons. I was still having a surge of direct marketing clients coming to me from all kinds of businesses. Yet I still didn't really understand the business of strategic consultancy and results. I just fumbled my way through until I got it right. No one ever noticed apart from me.

Looking back it was a crazy time yet a crazy time I loved.

Then this guy appeared on my copywriting horizon.

Michel Fortin

It all started at the Copywritersboard.com.

Michel Fortin is a brilliant man when it comes to words and I mean BRILLIANT.

Things change. When we first met online Michel had hair. He was also hugely unfit character. He was also a totally 'other-league' copywriter.

Today, he is fit, healthy, even more brilliant, but has lost all of his hair. He is one of the very few copywriters I admire for many many reasons. Anyway, let me share this with you.

Michel Fortin comes across as a reclusive, sensitive, shy and just perfect copywriter. He can be quite hard to get to know more fully. He is extremely genuine. I love him as a friend and mentor.

He is also the copywriter that owned the very early meeting place for copywriters over at copywritersboard.com that I mentioned earlier.

I don't remember exactly how I asked him, but I did ask him and he mentored me without actually mentoring me. I watched and read his work very carefully and simply copied what he was doing at the time.

I'll explain a little more.

For me, Michel Fortin is another-league as a copywriter. He is also an amazing strategic business mind. Like I mentioned I was part of his copywriter's board online. That's where we connected. I flirted now and then with him but I was also on the lookout for for someone to enlighten me more about this new world of copywriting. He was definitely in my radar.

I might not seem it, but I can also be pretty shy with new people and things. I'm a country, small village boy so can be reclusive also.

Anyway, I simply asked him if he needed help with his copy clients? He replied, not by saying yes but by sending me copy work. He always asked how fast can it finished? That actually freaked me out as I had no idea what I was doing. But I wanted to do it. Obviously I never once told that to Mike, I just said sure it'll be done for the following day, but rarely more than 2-3 days.

Mike also had a secret I had never seen before. I certainly hadn't used this with any of my writing clients. It was a way to prepare and make the copy easier. this secret was his incredible client questionnaire. Just a stroke of genius. OnCe the questions were filled out the basic foundations for the copy had been done. I had never seen anything like this before. At the same time I had created and perfected a consultation in the hairdressing industry so I then had that moment of wondering why on earth I hadn't been doing his with copy clients.

Another thing I learned was this; fail to do that question sheet and you usually pay very dearly.

A lot of the time Mike would be really pressed on deadline. I stayed up all night and did it despite having to get up, sort out my kids in the middle of the night and then leave home for 7:30am to make sure my salons were all open.

By the way this wasn't that easy as laptops weren't really happening in those days. I would take my state-of-the-art Pentium 90 (computer) to my office in the salon. The monitor was one of those horrible huge square white things, the tower was huge and there were always a million cables to sort out. Then at the end of the day I would take it apart and carry back to my car. Then once home I would wire the whole thing up again so I could carry on trying to finish these copy projects for Mike.

Anyway, once the copy was done I would email it back to Mike in Canada. He rarely replied to the copy I sent over to him (via dial-up,) but he would BCC me the finished copy a few days later as he sent it to the client.

This is the part I loved.

It was my letter, but the tweaks were just incredible. I never once failed to carefully study the subtle changes line-by-line. Some so subtle you would have to know the change. I could hardly believe the power adding or removing just one or two or three words could have. This was a revelation for me. Mike in my eyes a total genius when it comes to writing 'perfect' copy.

I would open my letter and go through each line compared to what Mike had sent over. It was a true masterclass in 'knowing' the difference with Mike and what he knew. I loved it.

My copy had been super-charged. The opening, the middle, the end, the close, the offer just the whole thing was incredibly masterful at so many writing and response levels. I was hooked. My new style of writing from that point was always based on a cross between Michel Fortin and David Ogilvy for a few years at least.

Once I had mastered my mentors teaching it was time for me to grow and keep developing as a copywriter with my own style. The truth is I wanted people to see my copy and say I bet that is Alan's. I was used to that with my hairdressing. People would ask if I had done so and so's hair. It was a style. I wanted a style to my writing also. There were lots of occasions that was starting to take place.

I just cannot write enough about Mike. Michel Fortin is a rare master of understanding words and an original when it comes to powerful word use as a higher response copywriter. He's like a Jedi, says little, but delivers in some kind of super power.

Michel has a word flow like no one else. His style and writing energy is always clean, honest, perfect, detailed powerful and unique to Mike. His style feels calm when it should be calm and is loaded when it needs to be fully loaded. I just wanted to be as good as him at this point.

He is just one of those greater, higher-ranked copywriters that I fully respect as integrity driven, truthfully compliant writer that displays strong ethics in his work.

And, get this, as I wrote copy for Mike he would pay me my cut and that was sometimes as high as $10,000 for writing sales copy.

Holy Shit!

Why the hell was I locked into the world of hairdressing and displaying indecision about leaving that world when I was earning money like this?

Michel also opened up a new world for me that I never really felt part of. This also opened up more doors and helped me prove myself as a great writer within the copy community. The copy community is a strange place. It is packed with individuals that shout too loud whilst telling everyone that they are the best. Yet, you rarely see what they are writing.

I feel it's much better and stronger to stay under the radar and just keep producing great work. Great work delivers great clients. I never needed the praise of a group of anyone. Yet, I loved the feedback I would get from Mike. It was what I needed to breakthrough into copy world.

I am not sure when this began with Mike. I will guess the year 2000, but maybe Mike will remember better than me. Either way Michel Fortin will always play a pivotal part in my journey as a copywriter and I for one am eternally grateful for that.

There was a second thing with Michel.

He had mastered the art of presentation very easy online. My website presentation was a mess. I had branded well, but been unable to make it look cool online. Again I simply followed Mikes steps and did what he was doing. He did his stuff in blue whilst mine was in FF3300 or orange. We both used Microsoft Front Page.

It wasn't just the writing it was also about handling this new sense of business. Don't forget I had been a hairdresser for 20-years. For me the transition made me a little nervous as it was the great unknown. I also had a young family to look after so failure just wasn't an option.

At the same time one thing I learned from having hairdressing salons was that I had to make sure I was always in the public eye. This meant there would be no break in my self-promotions or marketing for my new brand Orange Beetle.

Mike and myself did finally meet. We first met in London around 2005 and had dinner together. We were both speaking at an event together. We again met in New Zealand and went for dinner on top of the needle revolving restaurant. Since our first ever contact we remain friends to this day.

The time eventually came when I needed to do more of my thing alone. I like to be reliant on myself and a self provider, so I needed more of my own clients. Maybe 2-3 years after working with the brilliant Michel Fortin I moved forward on my own and started to seriously build my own copy business.

Now, How would I get in front of many new clients as fast as I could?

Here's how I got seen fast.

Give Me An Hour Speaking With Jay Abraham And I'll Do It

One day back in my salon I had a fax arrive from the Jay Abraham Group in London. They were trying to sell me a ticket to see Jay in London at London Excel Conference centre. It was a terrible fax/ad. I wanted them to know. I bravely called them and spoke to a guy called George. I told him the ad was terrible. He agreed and told me the ad had pulled zero sales.

I reacted and made him an offer. I told him I would create new ads that you can use time and time again if you give me an hour to speak at the Jay Abraham event in London. He replied, 'yes.'

I took their ad and basically used a salon format ad I already had. I changed the words and sent it back over. They resent the ad. The new ad sold 73 tickets the next day it went out. It eventually filled the event with around 2000 at just under £2,000 per head. I had my one-hour of presenting live to Jay's audience now booked.

I had done a ton of talks all of my life. I was an ordained minister of a fundamentalist faith for over twenty-years. I had passed through an intensive Bible school and was a fully trained speaker. I knew how to speak and of course as a hairdresser you could hardly shut me up.

But I had never presented to 500 guys wearing black and grey suits with ties. All looking deadly serious.

I thought it over and decided to wear some ripped jeans; motorbike boots, a purple velvet jacket and just be myself. This way I would stand out instantly. The other speakers all wore suits with a shirt and tie. That was the important bit sorted.

What could or would I talk about? Like I said I had done a ton of speaking in the past, but not really B2B stuff like this.

So I swiped the table of contents from a very famous book advertising book called Scientific Advertising. I simply turned the chapter headings into a PowerPoint, but used my own content based around my salon and handful of clients experiences.

I did the talk, the crowd loved it and incredibly one guy realised the table of contents were from that book. He pulled me up over it.

We both laughed!

Now something more about money.

35k, 50k and 50k From a Talk

Unreal!

From that one talk I had numerous clients approach me to create work for them.

A TV production company approach me from that talk. They paid me £35,000 to create a new campaign for them for a film trade magazine. The ads were all designed to position them as probably the most reliable film crew ever. They reported back the ads were a huge success.

I had two other high paying clients approach me from that presentation. Both paid me £50,000 each. I was flying. As time went forward there were more clients arriving from that talk years saying that they had seen me speaking at Jay Abraham event in London.

I had now earned more than a year's wage from just one client that came from a single talk. That's insane.

By the way, the film guys I mentioned above told me the first run from their new ad campaign had brought in over £250,000 of work per month! The last time time we spoke they were still running the same ads.

Going back a step I did mention two clients paid me 50k. One of those clients was a famous business author. He paid me 50k.

This was my first serious issue with a pain in the ass client.

And he was a pain in the ass!

The Fifty Grand Refund

It began like this.

"Alan, we are struggling to sell anything from our ads. We have never sold a thing online from any marketing efforts. Please help us to change that."

I had a gut feeling about this client from day one. So as crazy as it sounds I didn't cash the cheque. When ready, I sent over the first work and they complained saying it was different to what they had. I replied "of course it's different because this has been written to sell not simply inform."

They resisted the copy like crazy. I was confident they were wrong, because I had written a ton of copy at this point and felt like I knew what I was doing.

I wrote their web copy and a large email sequence for them. I also had started to work on their magazine and trade ads. They reported that the sales had begun to arrive almost instantly from the new copy.

Yet, they again complained saying the copy sounded nothing like their previous copy. I told them that is why you are getting sales because it is nothing like the old copy.

They then replied saying they want it more like what they had. This went on for around four weeks until I sent them a brown envelope.

Inside on one sheet of white A4 paper it said something like this.

"Enclosed is your uncashed cheque for £50,000. Please never contact me again."

They were furious and told me angrily over the phone. I was furious for my time lost and wanted to invoice them for that time. The experience in dealing with clients was invaluable.

Then a strange thing. Around 6-months later I received an email from them. It was from their son. He apologised for their behaviour and told me since the copy went back to the old copy sales had stopped stone-cold-dead. Would I be interested in taking on their project once again? I think today's term is LOL!

Clients can and do behave in strange ways that sometimes are not worth the brain time trying to work out.

Then this started happening.

Speaking Invites

I went to watch my son in his punk band playing a gig in high school. During the gig my phone started to vibrate in my pocket. I took out my phone and realised it was an American number by the dial code. I switched off the phone and thought they would leave a message. They did leave a message. It was a guy from the USA that had heard about my work from the Jay Abraham event and he wanted me to speak at his event in London.

I was flattered, but I didn't have time. The work Michel Fortin was sending me was becoming so much in volume I hardly had time to breath. My own leads, clients and work was even greater. My own SEO efforts online (way before paid search) had me placed on page one; position one of all major search engines. I couldn't check my email without a request for a quote or a simple request of, "we want you so how much?"

I also wanted more local work, so I decided to see if I could use lists from the local chamber of commerce. They insisted I first go to a breakfast meeting (I really don't do meetings like this at all) to meet and greet. Then and only then could I mail the group? I did that and then began direct mailing local businesses with the very same three-steps system I had mastered in my salons years earlier.

I did some local speaking gigs as well as the big gigs. The local gigs always paid me very very well. Mind you so did the big ones but I never really felt good about selling to a captive, hungry and mostly desperate audience.

The response to all of my efforts was always very strong and frankly I was never short of work. The big problem I was having was my salons were also keeping a tight hold on me. I decided to sell them, they sold. This was to my family's absolute dismay, yet my reality was I was getting paid huge amounts for consulting and writing.

So the speaking took off. USA, New Zealand, Latvia, Singapore and far more than I can write here. I'll tell you more about that in a moment.

Most of my work was pouring in from referrals, direct mail and now online forms and email.

And it was pouring in big time.

The Business of Being a Speaker

I have a lot of thoughts on speaking and speakers, but I will save them for another day or maybe another book (fiction would be a better book for that one.)

Speaking has always been good for me but I have a very fixed idea of what I wanted from my own speaking events. At my Bible school training we always had to create a talk that informed with an outcome and a desire action at the end of each talk.

All talks had to be themed and that theme had to be coherent from start to end. It was also critical I knew how the audience was thinking so I could tap into mind triggers and share with what they wanted to hear. But that was Bible talks. I used exactly the same methods with my business talks.

I would find out who was going to be there. What level of business people were they. But there was one thing I did that I never really saw any other speakers do and it was this.

I mostly looked for and found out higher-end clients or those that took their business far more seriously. The reason for this is I always felt my experience and proven history had been very high value so why should I give my high-value skillsets away for a low fee.

I took a speaking engagement in London. All of the speakers were offering a pitch that was very similar in sound and appearance. It was more about the sale. They would give a low content talk based on hopes and dreams and then offer the key to the kingdom at the end of the talk for say £1,995. Some of these guys were so good, so powerful, so convincing even I wanted to buy from them.

NOTE: The huge volume of refunds from the speakers at these events was staggering to see and hear.

I couldn't and wouldn't do that. So, I fully loaded my talks with extremely high-value content, shared my own office 'secrets' and tips and then would say at the end.

"I have one space for a client, the fee to work with me is £50,000." At one event I had three clients come to me and make that payment and commitment.

How?

I know as a copywriter that real business people want real value. By sharing my expertise I could also reveal my real value to the business owners listening. As a writer I also understand that copywriting is simply thoughts on paper. I simply tapped into what I thought the audience were thinking.

Earlier the story about the refund was one of those clients but the other two were more than happy and had results to shout about.

The accidental copywriter has arrived.

The U.K.s Number One Copywriter?

I don't and have never liked labels.

I find them restricting and they create an over expectation from others as to what they expected from me. Something had happened to me through doing a lot of presenting. The presenters never knew how to present me on stage so they would say things like… "The U.K.s number one copywriter…"

I never liked it because my own reality I am a business builder. Copy is simply part of the machine I use to build a business. You can have the most incredible copy that will never perform in a million years if the strategy or target is wrong. You can also have very average copy and an incredible result if the strategy and target is right.

The other issue with labels is they have a tendency to force people into playing a role. In my experience new copywriters seem to be living the role more than the skill of being a real copywriter these days. I had no interest in that. I was here to get paid … that's it!

However …!

This label was giving me what I needed at the time and that was a ton of clients and I mean a ton. It was also giving me a ton of money in the bank. It also handed me a certain amount of success in the world as a very high demand copywriter that was demanding high fees. That gave me some incredible and unforgettable doors to walk through that I just loved.

I do want to thank those that invited me to talk at their events.

At the start of this book I told you about Jay Conrad Levinson the genius that created the guerrilla marketing series was the only real encyclopaedic book I used, owned and referred to for my hair salon marketing.

Then this happened.

OMG JAY CONRAD LEVINSON

He was tiny.

I had been invited to speak in Atlanta, Georgia, in the USA by respected seminar promoter Armand Morin at his BigSeminar event. I was thrilled and of course accepted the invite. I was speaking on the stage with the likes of Brendon Buchard, Armand Morin, Jack Canfield and many other well known experts in their field.

As always when speaking I almost always wore a kilt and other Scottish identifiers as well as my endless orange colour (brand) references. It worked brilliantly well and believe me no one would forget me. After my talk (where I was trying to get Americans to understand my northern England mixed with faint Scottish accent) I stood at the back of the room sweating like a dog. People told me they loved my presentation and appreciated my effort flying over to share with them.

After I cooled down I stood there alone at the back of the room just thinking to myself about the event. Then a very small, very thin elderly man walked up to me with a huge smile across his face. I would guess he was 5'5". He looked frail. He was however full of life and wore a T-shirt that was camouflage green.

'Hello' he said, stretched out his arm and congratulated me on a wonderful talk. The man said to me my talk and presentation was the best he had seen from anyone in a very long time. He told me some other very nice flattering things and then stood quietly. I have to admit I was thinking what does this little guy know about this stuff.

THEN: I looked at his name badge and it had three words for me to read.

JAY

CONRAD

LEVINSON

He stood silent and smiling. Like a big kid I froze and said something really stupid.

"OMG, you're Jay Conrad Levinson", I proclaimed like a star struck teenager. He replied in his own quiet way, "Yes I am."

I then turned into some kind of babbling idiot for a minute or two. I told him, "I can't believe it's you. My whole life in business has brought me to this point and that is meeting with you."

I then explained to Jay that it was his groundbreaking and timeless book Guerrilla Marketing, his words, his writing and his mind that gave me success with my hair salons in the very early 90s.

I explained how his detailed and explained simple strategies and thinking had helped me not only build my salon business but my consultancy and copy business. He smiled once more and simply invited me for dinner that evening.

The evening at dinner with Jay and his wife was truly an amazing experience for me. We became friends for life. We talked, shared life stories, revealed similar histories and more. It was a real friendship that transcended age and distance and even conversation.

We met again in London where he invited me to be a presenter at his small gathering and again at a later date he flew into Manchester to visit me with his wonderful wife Jeannie where we had dinner and a very long night of conversation.

He insisted I should write a book with him. That is one big regret of mine is I never made the time to do that with him. Life just took over as life does.

The last time we met was in the winter of 2011 in Manchester. I was to meet him at a hotel just half a mile from my home. My car broke down so I walked over go meet him. It started raining and I arrived soaked. Then we had the most wonderful dinners. That was me, Jay and his wife.

It was only later I found out that Jay was dying. Then he passed away. I was so shocked I cried. I wrote a eulogy that was just a piece of words that came to me in his death. One year later I discovered these were the final words to be read to him at his funeral.

Life can be PROFOUND in the smallest of moments!

Copywriting had led me to this truly special point in my life. This was a real gift for me to meet one of the greatest modern-day strategists and marketing men in modern times. Was everything really accidental?

I loved Jay.

I admired Jay.

I just felt at ease with Jay.

I also had dinner with other greats but none as great as he was.

But weirdly;

I always knew I would meet him one day.

Texas, Jay Abraham, Henry 8th & Elton John

I received an invite from the USA from an amazing guy who had generated his first million from a sales letter I had written for him.

I was invited to attend a BBQ in Texas at his wonderful home. I of course accepted. Once I got there I was met with the world of copywriting like I had never seen before under one roof.

As I walked through the door John Carlton was standing leaning against the wall drinking a bottled beer and talking with Yanik Silver. There was well over 100 guests at this party. All big names, all respected and I was one of them now.

The biggest thrill for me was coming across another great of mine. I adored, loved and worshipped his book that I had read and followed in the early nineties. It was Jay Abraham. He was speaking with the new passed Chet Holmes.

Eventually we talked and he was just a very gentle, very soft spoken and very cool guy. It's funny how you can learn something in a split moment. I noticed how he leaned in and just listened. Only once I had stopped speaking did he say anything. I always loved Jay Abraham. It felt like a real wow moment. There was many others of course. It was an amazing moment for me.

The next day we all went fishing on the big lake. Fishing, eating, relaxing and just enjoying each others company. Thank you to Alicia for putting together something so amazing.

Back in England I had another invite to attend an exclusive party where Sir Elton John was the entertainment. I did say Sir Elton John. The invite invite in the mail. It was an invite to attend a birthday party of the brilliant marketing man Andrew Reynolds. Again he is just a totally brilliant direct marketer. I would say almost P.T. Barnumesque in his thinking and actions. I don't think I have seen anyone work direct mail the way he does it.

I had been invited to Hampton Court the home of King Henry 8th. This is where the party would be held. I decided to wear my kilt and dress up my very best for the occasion. I had put me on the table that was literally next to Elton's piano. I was sitting maybe ten feet or so away from Elton John as he played his hits for an hour or so. What an incredible evening. This ex-hairdresser had really transformed into something very different.

Strangely at this incredible peak of my new career that was also the last time I went out with my first wife and the last time I drank alcohol. She hated what

I was doing, but that's a whole other book. After that night we parted after 27-years.

I had more invites to travel around the globe and present what I know about direct response and results. One invite took me to New Zealand where I flew in, did my talk and flew out again. Travel time 36 hours! I'll share that in a moment.

OMG Elton John.

He never came in my salon.

What a thrill.

Corporate Chaos and The Big Desk

I remember it well. It was late on a dark winter's Sunday evening.

I received a frantic call from a large and relatively new company in London. They were looking to eventually float on the stock exchange. Everything they were doing with their approach to marketing just wasn't working. The marketing team had become obsessed with using LinkedIn despite the fact they never had any leads or clients from there.

This company was the biggest in the U.K. for their speciality. They wanted urgent help.

Now I can't share too much as I had to sign the official secrets act (literally) to enter the office building. I also had to promise no details of the company would ever be shared.

I sat down on the old English leather chair until my clearance came back. Once cleared I was taken to a huge room where the directors and myself chatted for maybe 30-minutes or more. They wanted me to help them increase numbers, leads, response and the voice of the business. I had come highly recommended.

After that initial meeting I had to meet all the partners and all of the marketing team and sales people. I walked along a very long corridor until we reached a huge room that looked like it had been fitted in the 1970s. It was wrapped in endless brown and chrome.

Next one by one they all arrived. Around the table I would say there was around 25 individuals. All were dressed in suits, sitting in front of laptops, pads, phones and more phones.

I sat there wearing a leather biker jacket, knee length vintage biker boots, tattooed and nose pierced. I could see by the look on their faces they were all thinking 'who the hell is this guy?'

And if I am being truly honest I was thinking "what the hell am I doing here. Help I want to leave." I will be absolutely honest for you. I felt hugely intimidated as something this big was new for me but my experience told me this. I had to be as cool as ice and show zero intimidation.

I sat calmly. I was then suddenly asked to host the meeting. I had zero prepared. All of them sat and waited for me to start. Pens at the ready. I nervously stood up, took control and told them to simply tell me what is going on and what they needed.

Then I sat back down (I was almost shitting my pants). The conversation then began, the blame game and the telling of the problem of each other rather than the actual problem.

Two words … CORPORATE CHAOS.

Another two words: EXPENSIVE CHAOS

Wages alone for a marketing team that was not delivering results was around one quarter of a million pounds annually. Can you imagine paying that amount of cash out for something that just fails?

I swear, I sat there and in that moment I realised this multi-million pound corporation was being run worse than any of my salons were ever run. Even I didn't have a clue what I had been doing in those salon days, but it just worked. This was a brutal unorganised, amateurish mess to say the least.

After spending a lot of time with them I went away. I then came back to them with a very detailed plan of what needs to be done. One thing I wanted them to do was to utilise their large email list.

This was a tiny part of the steps, but I knew we could create a result fast from existing contacts. They were terrified to email incase people complained.

I wrote a strong series of emails. These emails were to be delivered daily for two weeks.

This next bit is true; They insisted on large online conference meetings to discuss each email. I arrived online. I faced around eight faces over the call. The one to my left would say something. That something would then be passed down the line to the one at the other end on my right. They would reply and that reply would then go up and down the line.

After 20-minutes I told them I don't work like this and had to leave. It was chaotic.

After a few more discussions with the man at the top we finally agreed to hand control of the emails to me and I myself would do what is needed.

I sent the emails and here is what happened.

This results went from one lead a day to 17-leads per hour. The phone was literally blown off the hook. Staff were furious as they no longer had time to catch up and drink their coffee.

Now here is what was interesting. The campaigns began. After the phone and emails started going crazy their marketing manager asked for all of the new systems be be switched off as they couldn't handle the new volume.

This was a college graduated marketing team that appeared to love one lead a day and not seventeen leads per hour. This is what can easily happened when you leave things to so-called in-house experts.

The new magazines ads I had created were also converting like never before. I had redesigned their website, rewrote all of the copy and added a ton of simple tricks that I knew worked. Everything was now converting and the numbers were rising fast.

The one thing I had learned here was that despite what staff or employed experts say, unless they deliver on their promises they should be removed from their positions instantly. I also learned that the size of the company means nothing. I also discovered this. Unless you stay in control and work with a plan not a lot happens.

I would have fired that whole team and started again. They didn't do that and lost a huge contract as a direct result of that terrible team.

It was a crazy project for me. The little hairdresser now working with one of the world's biggest and most prestigious corporations. This was a long way from a cut and blow dry.

Looking back it was pretty amazing year with those guys. Although the money was also just incredible they did frustrate me to death with the endless need to take notes, actions plans and then spend up to 10-weeks action anything or to send emails on their own.

But …

Although I did initially feel I was absolutely way out-of-my-depth what I learned through punk rock and being a hairdresser applied here for a success model very easily.

Do things different.

Break the rules.

Do what you know is right.

Thank God I over-delivered.

And they knew it.

The Famous Groucho Club in Soho

£2,000 for a meeting.

Another email I received was from a guy name Brian Timoney. A really very nice guy. He and his wife had created a truly brilliant specialist company for method actors. They wanted advice on branding and positioning and general ideas for other directions.

My fee was £2000 for the meeting. They were happy to pay it. The location was London's famous members only club, The Groucho Club.

I went, we ate lunch. We talked strategies. We talked branding, ideas and more. They told me they had loved what I shared.

Years earlier when everyone had started to meet and do business in coffee shops I refused to do that. I knew I wouldn't want a serious meeting in a coffee shop for my own business so why would my clients? I wanted to be taken seriously and that including meeting in locations that reflected the high-end, the quality and the premium services I offer. This was a perfect location and set the scene for a perfect meeting. If you want to become an actor Brian is definitely your man.

Let's not forget.

£2000 for a single meeting. This was 'Alan the hairdresser' in a brave new world that used to earn around £25 per hour after deductions. I had to work out how to do this and I did it. Premium has a fee and I was offering and presenting premium at all times.

And I was honoured to meet at the very cool Groucho Club - loved it!

Again, I was always asking myself questions. How did this ex-hairdresser end up in one of London's most famous members only clubs eating fully paid lunch whilst getting paid what felt like 100-times more than when I was a hairdresser - for a 3-hour lunch meeting.

After lunch I rushed back to Euston station and grabbed the last train home.

I can tell you I sat on that train home wondering how I managed to get to this point.

The two grand in my pocket felt great!

Cyprus Mobsters

Is that an AK47?

I had been invited over to Cyprus to recover from divorce by an acquaintance (now friend.) In return I was asked to offer some advice to help out this client with one of his businesses. Once I arrived I was told not to cook for myself because he and his wife would cook for me everyday until I went back home. I could stay for as long as I wanted.

His name is Jarl. He was very nice and very genuine to me although I really didn't know him all that well at this time. He gave a Mercedes sports car, a nice motorbike and a very large home to use for as long as I wanted to stay.

This was a four bedroomed house with just me in there. He really was a total gentleman. All he wanted in return was some advice. I think deep down he wanted to help me through my divorce. He'd read about it online.

One evening I went over as per usual to his house just across from where I was staying. Dinner wasn't quite ready. We sat by the pool and talked. I was told some other guests were also going to show up.

I was also told not to be nervous about these guys when they arrived. They were apparently really nice guys and would show no interest in me apart from the usual 'hello.'

Four guys walked in. I mean four tough guys. They looked wild. They put a large holdall on the table. They opened up the holdall and pulled out guns - real guns!

Three carried handguns and then took out what looked like an AK47 on a shoulder strap. The three guys then posted themselves around the gated property whilst one guy sat and spoke to my host and client. They wanted to know who I was. I said nothing, my client explained who I was and then they just ignored me.

I just sat next to the pool in silence. It was a bit weird, but it felt ok. I had no idea what was going on. Later after they left I was told was they had survived the Bosnia war with prices on their heads. Thankfully they really didn't stay that long.

I can tell you that was a moment I wished I was doing a haircut again.

Sadly, I found out later that Jarl's beautiful wife had died very young and left Jarl alone looking after his kids.

This copywriting was filling my life story book with all kinds of stories and experiences. I had resigned myself to accept everything as it was for now.

Not everything is about money.

Read this.

Alan, You Saved Her Life

I had just gotten off a flight from Manchester, U.K. to New Zealand. I flew in and then got back on a plane and flew all the way back home after this talk. It was truly exhausting.

But, this was a very special experience for me for this reason. I had spoken in Sydney, Australia a few months earlier and had been seen and heard by a women in the crowd. She went away and applied what I had been talking about. She made money but not money to buy stuff. She had come to see me in New Zealand and explained everything.

After I came off the stage after my talk this same woman found me and asked for a minute. She told me that she had seen me speaking in Sydney and loved what I had spoken about.

After my talk in Australia, she went her way home and put into practice what I had been showing and teaching about copy, words and mind triggers. She then told me that after doing what I had shown the audience she had managed to raise enough cash to pay for a lifesaving heart operation on a young girl. Then she cried, hugged me, thanked me for helping to save the life of a young woman I clearly had never met." Alan, it was you that saved her life."

I cried. I was dumbfounded. It was just an incredible moment for me.

This woman had jumped on a plane and flown from Australia to New Zealand just to say thank you to me personally. I couldn't believe it.

I have clients that have never once said thank you and they live close by. This was an amazing and very real human moment.

The impact words can have on another life should never be under estimated or abused.

As I was about to discover.

I Wrote My Wife Into My Life

I first saw my wife in London in 2009.

A beautiful woman approached me before a speaking gig. I was standing alone. She came up to me on her own and asked if I was Alan Forrest Smith. I replied yes. She told me her name, said hello in her beautiful accent, then she shook my hand and then walked away.

I went on stage. I was speaking and noticed she sat on the front row. She was wearing a red jumper and black skirt. Her hair was long and she had a very foreign look about her. She was beautiful. I couldn't help looking at her as I was talking (I know that sounds weird.)

Today she is my now wife. My wife is from the Tbilisi, Republic of Georgia, but lived in London. After I saw her and asked her full name I looked her up on Facebook and friend requested her.

Now, I have no idea about dating as I had never really dated anyone apart from my first wife from the age of 15-years old. So I thought about what she was posting on her Facebook but never made comments to her posts. I wanted to grab her attention.

I realised she like Led Zeppelin and posted their videos now and then. Not only did I not like them it was a very punk rock thing to be anti 70s rock bands.

But, I was attracted to her big time and wanted to grab her attention so had to make an exception. One day she posted 'stairway to heaven.' I made a comment a bit like… " I love that song, love Led Zeppelin and it's one of my favourite videos. It wasn't, I had never actually heard the song and knew zero about Led Zeppelin. But I knew she would love to hear that comment. She liked what I wrote (words) so I had urgently rush away and learn some Led Zeppelin tracks.

I began writing my stories and words to her until we eventually fell in love, got married and of course had our son darling son in 2019, our little Demna.

But the point is this.

If I wasn't a writer and simply had to talk the date through I would probably never been able to bring her into my life.

I really did write my wife into my life.

Thats the power of good copy.

Later on I wrote our New York wedding in 2015. Once the wedding was planned I created a campaign that would give us the cash to be able to pay for the flights, buy rings, pull the whole wedding together.

That's a whole other story.

That's also a true story.

Of course, if she reads this.

"Darling I love you forever, you are my woman."
I'm a big softie at heart.
I think you'll know that by now.
Speaking of speaking - again.

Speaking And Classes … Maybe, Maybe Not

I did my first public speaking gig at hairdressing college in Manchester.

Actually come to think about it my first stage speaking was 1979 with my punk band.

Back to the college; I was the one to begin the presentation in front of hundreds of people. It was a national college competition. Once the team and myself got up on stage I was about to speak when someone pointed out my trousers zip was down and my white shirt tail was poking out of the zip. I fixed it, I was embarrassed, I lost my train of thought and completely froze on the spot. We finished the competition last.

From 1985 onwards I attended a Bible school for speaking. I attended that school for just over twenty years. It was every Thursday evening at 7:15 pm. It was thorough in every last and tiny detail. From breathing to projection to posture. I loved that school - LOVED IT! I attended weekly for those twenty plus years.

I had also spoken on stage for businesses, at groups and had done a lot of speaking in the hairdressing world for well known cosmic companies to hundreds of hairdressers.

I once got invited and went to Latvia for a four-day trip, all expenses paid to speak to over 1000 hair salon owners. They were struggling to breakout of the post-communist mentality. Every time I spoke they then the translator translated my words. That was before Alan the copywriter appeared.

This new marketing and 'desperate to be a speaker' world was very alien to me. The speaking badge or gig appeared to be a big dream of many of these new marketers and copywriters.

I had personally been speaking for decades before as an ordained minister. I had been trained to speak the truth based on actual provable facts, trained to help others and trained to share words from the Bible.

The art of speaking and sharing was to be taken extremely seriously and never to be abused. That felt embedded into my DNA. The influence and prestige of an expert on stage can be huge to those listening. The listeners trust a speaker. That should be respected. Although I had left that faith after twenty-years the principles of speaking as an expert from a platform never left me.

I had now been invited to speak all over the globe. I spoke to well over 30,000 people. I loved it. I hated it. I was confused by it. I didn't like the trapping and selling aspect. It felt dishonest on so many levels.

Speaking at this level definitely wasn't for me in these high-pitch forums at this time as a copywriter. It felt as though the whole idea was to fill an arena with as many lost or desperate people as possible and then sell them as much as possible to make as much as possible.

Money with a sale was always king and rarely service given to the buyer. The punk hadn't left me. The punk ethic always had a naive honesty. I still think I'm like that today.

I had seen speakers sell literally millions from a single talk. Some were selling banned software or services that I knew wouldn't in a million years work in the real world. I once watched a speaker take well over one million in sales from stage. He had laughed and joked in the backroom that all of his online accounts had been banned and currently didn't have any working software. He also joked that most would never use it anyway. I found and find that shocking abuse of power.

It just didn't feel good for me to be part of this. I was no longer a minister yet I felt that strong conscience and sensitivity that hadn't really left me. I decided to pull back from speaking as a way of making extra money.

I also know and recognise there are still amazing speakers out there that add massive value to the lives of others. Not all are bad.

This taught me a lot about this new world I was now part of. It really wasn't what I wanted or what I set out to achieve with my copywriting, consulting or writing.

I still had the urge to sit and write, write, write and write books. A lot of this 'other stuff' like speaking had too many major distractions on my mind and time.

I wondered about doing some master classes teaching and sharing what I knew about what I knew. It wasn't writing rather moving into the teaching arena. I did many, but they gave me no real lasting satisfaction apart from the initial adrenaline and of course great cash. I also did them with some truly great guys.

Like my hippy, ex-cult member and Californian Italian pal Tim who died suddenly from a brain tumour. I loved that guy it was an honour to know him.

He was the most gentle man. He was the most brilliant copywriter.

My Copywriters Masterclass 2005

This was a pivotal moment for me. I had never really taught anyone to write anything after all I really never thought of myself as a writer or copywriter even at this stage. Almost all that attended my 2005 copywriters masterclass class felt incredible impact on their business or their copy skills. Even today those I have contact with are still using the benefits.

After day one of my copywriters masterclass and going through the detail behind headlines, offers and some other things, one guy - Kevin - went back to his hotel room and wrote an email using what he had discovered during the class.

He told me had been emailing his business list for years. The business was now very close to folding. His emails had always failed. His cheap often confusing offers had totally confused the list and also confused my client's mind on what is the best way to send out mailers and emails.

Kevin told me that overnight he had applied everything to the email he'd written and sent it. He made sweeping changes to every single word and the way the offer was constructed. The next morning in the class he approached me with a huge smile. He then shared his overnight story of success with me.

That success was actual sales of just over £42,000 from a single email that he had created overnight. All on the direct response principles I had shared with him were the same principles I had been using in my hairdressing salons all of those years earlier.

I shared Kevin's overnight success with my class. As you can imagine the atmosphere was now electric amongst the class of 27 new copywriting students.

Later after that class Kevin stayed in contact. His new skills as a copywriter had now netted his business well over a million. Don't tell me words don't make a difference.

Another guy at that class Steve who wanted to become a copywriter. He had flown in all the way from Sydney to join me. He later reported that in just 12-weeks he had taken and banked invoices for over $90,000.

It might sound easy, but don't forget even this far into the book that I had changed my whole career and life from hairdresser and was now proudly a copywriter.

I had many days, letters, pages and campaigns where I endlessly doubted my work. Unlike today's new copywriters that go on and on about how amazing they are, I just never felt that way. I always wanted more. I always wanted to get better. I always wanted to write better, stronger and bigger.

Confidence and ego live in different house. I knew which one was mine. I really don't think that has changed.

Yet I still do what I do.

I still get my results.

And, I used to be a hairdresser.

Work And Not Work

At this stage I could pick and choose as many or as few clients as I wanted to work with. Fees? I was getting money thrown at me and could ask as much as a £100,000 anytime I wanted and I was getting it.

The result was a fact driven and proven consultant, copywriter, and strategic brain doing as much or as little as I wanted to do. I was earning very – very – good money from mainly just writing and advising.

I adjusted my work time right down to 3-days a week. Each work day was as long or as short as it needed to be. My priority was servicing my clients, but also creating a life I needed on my terms. I also need to write and always get better. Second never feels like a good position for me. I had to be number one where I could be number one.

Writing as a copywriter - despite being accidental - changed every aspect of my life. In the salons I had easily worked 7-days a week with very long days stuck to the same depressing building. I had been getting paid less than my top staff and they were working far less hours than I was.

But this new way was very different. The punk ethic was all about freedom and this gave me the freedom I always crave inside. I always need to be able to create my life on my own terms. Life was now a long way from the salon days.

I had been around the globe so many times. From Australasia, to Asia, too beaches in Malaysia to the crazy streets of Singapore and many, many others.

But you should know this.

It was hard work, but the type of hard work that delivered rewards I wanted and I could adjust as I needed to adjust them.

I know you'd love to know more stories, but honestly there were just so many it is hard for me to sit here and put all of them down. What I will say is my transition had been more than complete. I felt like a new version of myself had finally been released and life was now very different.

Not everything went well. A divorce after 27-years. A abandonment of a 20-year faith. A humiliating bankruptcy brought on by that destructive divorce. All took place during these times. Some of it my fault, some if it not. Let's be honest it's hard to have a fight alone right?

Talking of faith.

God Had Gone

I know this is about the accidental copywriter. I feel my faith had a huge part of me understanding words and minds. I want to share this small part of the story as I think it's critical.

After twenty-years plus as an ordained minister, going to meetings everyday of the week, praying, reading, studying and a ministry. After that had gone I felt an overwhelming sense of loss.

It felt like a real death. It felt like a totally catastrophic event. It felt like my purpose to my life had now gone. I felt totally unworthy. I now lived in a black void. Finding my true self wasn't going to be easy.

It wasn't.

But found myself.

I had been there all along. I just had to release my true character from the decades of self-imposed and blindly accepted layers.

In a strange way this was the moment I was really free to write. Yet I missed my relationship with God.

Maybe I will explain more one day in another book.

But life continued and life has never been better than it is right now.

Becoming an accidental copywriter had looked after me, given me a very good life and shown me a skill I never for one minute realised I had inside.

Despite the hiccups, life was back on track and flying once again.

It is great to be alive.

Although the question of God never leaves me for a single day.

Does it leave anyone?

Opportunity Rarely Travels By Twice

My first wife embarrassed me once in the most humiliating way.

I met an old pal from school that knew me as the hairdresser. He asked me what I am up to? I proudly told him I was now a writer. My first wife spoke up in a second and said in front of him, "no you're not you're a hairdresser".

Funny right? Not really because I am a very sensitive type and could have easily stopped writing copy after that comment. Maybe at heart I was still a hairdresser? But my truth was I hadn't cut hair for a few years at this point.

When people tell you something about yourself it is usually about themselves and reveals more about them than you. This could have derailed me if I had allowed it to.

You see at the start of this journey I could have easily said so many times this isn't for me. I am uncomfortable doing something new. I don't want to do it or I can't do this. I don't know why I just went with the flow despite strange family oppositions. Of course I never did anything I didn't believe I could do but there was a point where I was wondering where is all this coming from.

Looking back there were one or two things in my life I didn't grab by both hands but I really should have grabbed them. But that's fine. I realise now that life is like that. When opportunity comes along it can be so easy to find an excuse to say no.

The problem is opportunity rarely passes by twice. Oh well.

Words and Accountability

Words really do have consequences. The money should always come second. The service or filling the need genuinely should come first. But even more – the absolute truth is king and should conquer all things. I see so many copywriters saying what sounds good, reads great or just increases persuasion for the sale. The truth is an after thought.

I trained a young writer. He sent me his sales page for review. On his page it said he was an A-grade copywriter and a master in persuasion. I confronted him and asked him if these things are true? He replied 'no' but if I say less they won't hire me. He was neither of those things. In fact he hadn't worked in a job at this point. The only person he ever persuaded was his mother and father to buy him new phones and gaming machines.

That was foolish. I certainly didn't train him that way. He let his fear overtake his skillset. Fear of not being hired.

I don't like the idea of that being done to my wife or my kids or my family so why would it be fine to do to others? As a writer I want to be accountable and I want to be measured for the truth. If I have written it I want to stand-by what I have written.

In a world where significance, glory and ego have become king a need for truth has been pushed to the side for a need to be recognised as the best (even without the efforts). I realised early that would be the last thing I wanted but it can be easy to get swept up in the hype.

The written word.

It still has respect. It is still respected. It is still believed and accepted as a fact. What we write has created the sentence. The sentence is the same as when the judge makes his final summary and writes his final sentence. The written word should be held the highest point and stood by at all times. If we have no respect for what we write and we start to write things for mass persuasion we have broken down a barrier that might be hard to rebuild. For me it is critical that the written word is always respected and held on to.

The written word is still king.

I am a believer.

My Powerhouse Three Letter System (6-steps with lift note)

I know a few of you reading this will be wanting to know more about my three letter system I mention so often and used time and time again with my clients.

I first did these letters maybe around 1992 in my salons. Not for any reason it just seemed obvious.

I thought the whole process of sending and receiving through from the client perspective and realised this.

They might get the first letter and just not react. They might get the second letter and think about reacting.

They might read the third letter and start to take more attention.

That was it.

So my first letter usually read a little like an introduction and an offer.

The second letter would be more of the same with a new headline and an even better offer.

The third letter would still be a similar letter to the previous letters one and two but the offer would go to right to the edge.

In other words, the offer would have to be completely irresistible. All letters would have a 3-day act now offer closes-by date. (important)

I would send all three letters and wait for the results.

Send letter one. Send the next 5-7 days later. Send the third 5-7 days later. I would repeat the whole process sometimes monthly.

The clients that reacted were removed from the list and those that didn't react I would resend the same three system a month later.

This time each letter would have an addition. That addition was a lift note. The lift note would summarise the whole letter but would also have a sense of urgency attached to the note.

So actually my three letter system was six letters with lift notes.

Also worthy of note.

I would send and resend these letter for years - not months (or just once). Until they client receiving the letter would physically tell me not to send I would still send.

Is that spam?

No. Apple advertise everywhere. Is that spam? No one will know about your great business unless you tell them how great your business really is.

I have used this format for

Hairdressers

Landscapers

Security companies

Real Estates

Goldsmiths

Golf companies

Fitness clubs

Yoga clubs

In fact, hundreds of my clients and businesses including my own.

There are some rules.

Rule 1: It isn't just about your great copy. It is always about the target market. Remember earlier when I mentioned to you I knew my salon clients would look into the mirror at home and say to themselves, "when's the last time I changed my hair?" That's what the target market is thinking. Break that rule if you know a better way(at your own risk).

Rule 2: Make sure you speak in a language they are speaking in already. Avoid introducing new words they aren't familiar with. Find the exact words they use. These words are the emotional reaction triggers that enable the reader to attach themselves to the copy and the story around the copy. It's empathetic writing. It's also a magnetic attraction for the mind to be drawn to it's already internal conversation. Break this one and you'll fail.

Rule 3: Spend hours, days, weeks on the top of the page or the headline. I labour so much over this part. It must have the product, the angle, the offer, be curious with an emotive grabber and give them enough 'want' to keep on reading. Drive the benefits hard. I once spent six months writing copy for a one client. I re-wrote just under fifty versions of the same advert with different headlines and top. SIX MONTHS! If you know a better way I dare you to break the rule.

Rule 4: Create a layered and value stacked offer that they will find impossible to refuse. I mean absolutely impossible. Especially if this is a first time client. I like to give new clients everything to get them in. The money is made after that first sale not with that first sale. Do you know better? Break the rule and show me different.

Rule 5: Time is precious, do what you know works or has worked elsewhere. Don't be a fool and spend forever trying to create something brand new. The chances are it will fail. Humans like familiarity. That also applies to reading habits like mailers or any other kind of reading. Use good swipes or good proven experiences to make sure your system works. If you don't like this rule, go on break it and see what happens!

Rule 6: Design the letter and take the design seriously. Use colour, get the fonts right, use high-resolution images, use columns, use side notes, add factoids, add expert opinions, just add what the market expects.

I'm a huge fan of imagery. It works. Make sure the envelope is also designed properly. I spend at least two weeks formatting my letters. Break this rule and you're crazy!

Rule 7: If your mailer fails that is fine. I usually mail 100 list names to test response. If that response is good I then mail the whole list. If not I take time to change the words and make adjustments. (some subtle) Some campaigns do and will fail. Use what you learn from the failure to create your best campaign ever. That's another rule for you to break

Rule 8: If you don't know what to do, find out what to do from the very best. Durgh!

Rule 9: If the offer is costing you money to get the result - build in the cost of the client. When the offer is created this way there should be a follow-up product or what marketers call a back-end. So create an offer they just cannot say no too. And if they do say no make them think they are insane. Only ignore this rule if you want to reduce your response. What you don't want to? Break it and you will.

I am a rule breaker as you probably realise by now. Yet when it comes to business I cannot afford the risk or failure. I like to reduce my risk as low as possible. That means following a few rules that have rarely failed me with my punk band, with my salons, with orange beetle, with writing love letters to my wife and for my clients.

I really really really don't like rules, but these are a few I would stick to.

Honestly, the biggest problem you will have is my three step/six step letters (with a lift note) system sounds so simple you might not want to try it.

And believe me I have met a lot of crazy clients that have actively torn this system apart, lost money doing that just because it all sounded too easy.

They forget.

Having a conversation is easy.

I have a client that has a large Yoga company. When we began working together maybe 10-years ago now she had zero response from anything she was sending to her lists. After looking at what she had been using in her marketing messages I realised that she had come from the corporate world and was using corporate words. She was also nervous about sending email or mail.

I researched, I found the right conversational words. I set up the systems and finally I helped her to relaunch. In under two weeks her business had pulled in bookings for her retreats of around $117,000.

How?

By doing exactly what I have just explained to you about. This is pure gold for any copywriter.

And a side-note: I still send out direct mail today. It stands out in today's noise. When done incredibly simple but well the results can be huge.

I currently have a three letter system I send to my hairdressing lists. That delivers around 25% response. That is sales every time we send it out.

I've just reminded myself I haven't sent it for a while.

I'll get that done after I write to you.

If you want money in the bank, letters still work and out perform most other gimmick marketing trends.

You Must Write Daily

Swimmers swim everyday.

Footballers kick a ball everyday. Racing car drivers drive cars everyday. That's how you get better than good. Practice is critical. So many writers only want to write if they get a client. I find that shocking. I also find it shocking they do that and expect or claim to be brilliant a-list copywriters.

My writing habit is daily. I write at least 2-3000 words every single day without fail. Today as I finish I have written over 5,000 words. This has served me well and fined tuned my skills as a writer a copywriter and a thinker. I have created literally thousands of blogs and and written over twenty books. If I guessed I would guess I write over a million words every year for myself. Then of course I write for clients.

A writer cannot be a writer if he or she doesn't write daily. If I don't write for a few days it is so easy for my own writing to get rusty and reduce in quality. Writing daily is critical for the success of a writer.

Read biographies or histories about real writers is also essential. Understand the mind and you will understand the technique of the writer. That raises the question who or what should I read? I can share what

I read for you. Tolstoy, Dostoevsky, Chekhov and other great writers.

But Alan they are not copywriters? True, but like I said to be great you have to follow and copy greatness. When it comes to words these are the very best. And copywriters? David Ogilvy, John Caples, P.T. Barnum were my heroes in my early copywriter's days.

There is only one modern day copywriter whose work I think is amazing and would read and that is the brilliant Clayton Makepeace. I know there are more I just don't have time to find them.

Did you write today?

Will you?

It's Broke So Offer To Fix It

It's broke so they come to us to get fixed.

Writing copy is also about fixing problems using words. If you fix a client's problem you will become the go to guy to fix those problems.

Problem: I need more leads.

Solution: I can help you by changing your message.

See how easy that was?

Most copywriters have the mindset that tells them they are there to write copy. That is completely wrong. Copy is the last thing the client wants. The client wants you to fix their problems and if you use copy in that process that is great.

A client came to me and asked for a 12 page sales letter with 350 words per page. I asked him why. He told me he'd read somewhere 12-pages were best. I tried to advise him otherwise. He wouldn't budge. He was adamant. I refused the client. Why? That isn't what he needed, he needs more response, increased results, he needs sales not copy. The number of pages won't make any difference. Copy is part of the process, but when a client starts to tell you what to do, in my experience, it is doomed to fail. After all they are not experts that is why they came to you in the first place.

I'd never go to a dentist and tell him how to fill my tooth would you?

So, you need to think bigger, broader and more expansive because if you just choose to just write copy like any other copywriter you are just a choice rather than the only option.

Work hard to find out the real problem of the client and just fix it – if you can. If you can't, get good and tested advice. I have copywriters coming to me all the time to help them fix their clients problems. It's not a sin, it's smart.

This next bit is an absolutely true story.

This client wanted it fixed and then got abducted by aliens (I think.)

I got a new enquiry, followed through, did what I need to do and then as always with my questions etc. Then I invoiced and had my £9,000 quote paid in advance.

I asked the client to send me what I needed and I prepared some research. The research at this early stage probably took me 15-minutes (once on a project I can spend up to weeks researching.)

One week passed and I heard nothing back from him. Two and three and four weeks passed and still nothing. I emailed him a few times to follow-up his payment of £9,000 into my bank.

Two months, three months and then well over a 6-months had passed. I still heard nothing.

In fact I heard nothing at all. I called and got no pick-up, I emailed and had no response. It was as if the guy had fallen off the edge of the planet.

I never heard from the client (who never actually became a client) and he never got back to me for a refund or an explanation. That was the easiest but most confusing £9,000 I ever got paid!

Maybe he had been abducted by aliens!

My Jay Abraham Confession

Please remember - I love Jay Abraham. My marketing grew mature with his work. Getting Everything You can From Everything You've got' is a must read book of his. But in this occasion I got a little greedy (in my favour the demand for my skills was pretty high at this point.)

So, I received an email and a phone call from a partner of Jay Abraham.

Despite my earlier brushing shoulders with him we never became close working partners or anything. But I would have loved to have had that with him during these busy times.

One his his venture partners asked me for a quote for sales copy. This was maybe 2006. I had gotten a little arrogant (maybe - probably) and sent back a minimum fee of £25,000. More like, "this is my fee pay or or go away cause I'm great" (probably.)

They wanted to pay me in commissions only. I had been asked that a million times over the years and tried it a few times to my great bank balance regret.

I replied no, it's £25,000 or nothing after all this was going to take at least three months of my time.

They replied the commissions would have come to well over £100k and I still replied "no."

Was this a mistake after all this was Jay Abraham and I would have sacrificed my life to do the best job ever?

Yes and no. I did learn early on to know my value and my price and never budge. I learned never to steal away from that. But the reality was I had missed a golden opportunity to work with a great that had passed my way, reached out to me and I pulled back my hand. I also learned that never take a risk on a new business for commissions only. I also knew the risk was as good as zero.

But this was Jay Abraham. He wasn't a new business. He was a marketing god of sorts. He was also a secret mentor of mine. I had discovered so much from his book mentioned above. I was a little shit in this moment.

I feel like a complete dick telling you that!

But, I'm ok with that.

LOL. DURGH. OMG!

Well I'm just a human and none of us are perfect. Sometimes we just get things wrong. I think I had become a slight victim of my own success at a certain level.

Anyway.

Maybe.

The still sun rises in the morning.

One Client Mindset

I am a one person person.

I once dated two women at once. Neither knew until they found out. They both wanted to kill me. I quickly realised that I am a one person person.

When one-client focused I think I am the perfect partner. Even I would pay for my madness when I am like this. If I feel perfect they get perfect work from me.

I thrive on one client. I want to partner with them. I take it all so seriously. I even dream about their business. I wake-up make notes and become a little obsessed when with one client. Their business becomes my business. I'm all a little over-the-top, but I work best like this. It energises me and turns me into an ideas machine. It's like fruit concentrate, I just go hyper for the project. It is how I like to work because in my own businesses that's how I always worked. It keeps me super-focused and helps me to over-deliver my very very very best.

I am always amazed how many copywriters cannot find a single client or are happy to post in groups and forums hoping to be the one that gets chosen. Even once chosen they seem happy to deliver for just like $500. I don't get that.

In the U.K. alone we have over five million businesses. All of them need a copywriter. That means there are truck loads of jobs for copywriters and plenty of work for freelance copywriters. If you go and get it. If you know how to go and get it.

If a copywriter isn't getting clients there is a reason for that. Mostly those reasons are they have learned how to write copy but failed to learn and master the true art of direct marketing.

For me it has never been an issue. In over three decades working from OrangeBeetle.com I have never once had a drought of clients. Yes, there is the odd slow period but never once has OrangeBeetle.com let me down.

It isn't uncommon for me to earn well over six-figures and more for a single project. Even then the client will usually have a windfall they never expected and are thrilled to see rolling in.

I do get asked how I do this and the answer is easy. I think I create great work and my clients seem to agree. My work has a hard-earned, proven reputation. My work is highly-polished, well thought out for angles and approach and finally very carefully put together. This attracts new clients rather than having to pursue hunt them down.

More critically, I also do my own direct marketing for my own businesses DAILY! Why daily? I know if I am not being seen and heard everyday I am soon forgotten. I learned in my salons the minute I switched off my marketing because we were too busy a drought of the flow of clients could soon take place.

A day never passes without me doing something to build my business.

NEVER!

But working with one client at a time empowers me and them.

Here's How I Write My Copy

There's no formula.

Don't be upset and don't resist, it's just a fact based on three decades of proof.

Yes there are things I do but I would hardly call it a formula. I would always call it the conversation and that's it.

Headline, yes.

Body, yes.

Stories, tons of them.

Facts, as many as possible.

Call to action, obviously.

But hardly a formula. I think the formula method comes from selling the formula method rather than getting specific results. Anyway here's my non-formula formula.

Before I get started writing any copy I usually do something like this. I need to know everything about the buyer or target. I need to know exactly how they think and why they think what they think. I want to know what they are talking about and what the conversation is. This is always the basis for my writings.

Then I do my initial research online. This can be as deep as I need to go. I also like specialist magazines, websites and groups for deeper research.

I focus on what customers are moaning about, problems they have and the help they ask each other for. Why? People buy solutions not problems.

My whole process for writing copy is based on ideas and observations – not writing. For me writing is the final piece of what I am doing.

So, I have to take time researching, thinking, observing, exchanging ideas, looking up ideas, going through ideas and more.

I will gather pages of notes. I like to do this on paper not digital. Paper is seen and felt and carries more dimensions. Digital is detached and easily out of sight. I like my desk a mess with the paper. I gives me a buzz that somethings happening in front of me. It's like building a house and watching the foundations go down before the walls.

I also gather all the historical ads if available from the client. I love to see the stuff that isn't working. This can tell me more than most once I have researched the buyer.

I will let this researched material sit in my mind as long as it needs to sit in my mind. I'll go for coffee, play guitar and do just about anything rather than write.

Then one day when I feel ready I write (that day isn't planned it just arrives.) I mostly write the copy out in one go. That can be a single page or 37 pages. I just write it out until it's done. For me this is always my very best copy. This is not finished copy. This is just the start for me. If I don't finish it on day one I will carry on early as on day two. Failing to do this can break flow and tone of the conversation. No edit or checks are done during this initial write.

I will then review the words, line by line, word by word the next day and then leave it for a few days so I can think it all through and really let it settle in my mind.

One thing I should mention is this. I can spend days and weeks and months on the big angle, the headline and the big idea. This means I will write many many headlines and then spend more days editing down the headlines until I have one (or two) very powerful headlines that say everything about the copy about to be read.

I would guess 98% or more of my effort and work goes into headline, big idea and the angle. That is a big one and very important one for me. Read again if you don't believe me. Now read again.

"98% or more of my effort and work goes into headline, big idea and the angle."

My training and work with copywriters always reveals that most copywriters write the headline last. This is a huge mistake. It is like building a house with no foundation. I actually think it is catastrophic to take this route.

Maybe this goes back to my Bible days or punk band days. That moment when you know you must get the point across. I loved titles like Anarchy in the

U.K. It said everything in just four words! I also love titles like REVELATION ... the power of that single word! I want to write like that. I think I do write a bit like that. That takes time and thinking and of course mastery of thought.

I then go back and do a big edit my copy(I hate this laborious bit but I do it.) My copy has to be themed (the angle). This means the start, the middle, the stories, the whole read show be one coherent and fluid piece. A big start, a strong middle, believable and true stories and a climatic end.

Editing a piece of copy isn't my thing; I have an advert in my files. I wrote around forty-fifty variations of that one advert. I could have done edits - I don't and I didn't. I think edits break the flow. So I didn't tweak it, edit it or change single lines. I rewrote the whole thing from the start with fresh eyes. (this is why group copy usually fails miserably.) The multiple voices might look good on paper but read terrible in the mind.

This gives me a feeling of coherence, flow, conversation and stability in my writing. I feel it is the perfect and most natural conversation. And then and only then do I share that copy with a client. I never send copy to a client that is half done or half hearted.

I also insist from my clients there is no time limit on delivery. I insist there is no feedback from office amateurs or un-specialised people.

And this is what attracts clients to me. They know I deliver far more than what most writers or copywriters can deliver. Again for me it isn't about writing, it's about thinking first, writing second.

How about you?

Do you just sit and write your copy and that's it? That's what almost every copywriter appears to do when I ask them. If that is what you do you are in a weak position. That will not deliver your best copy ever for a client or a project.

I don't search for clients these days, but when I did I would break every possible rule and do everything I could to get that client. What are you doing?

If you are doing what everyone does you will fail. If you create your own way of doing things you have a higher likelihood to succeed.

As long as ... you are creating great copy of course.

But of course you have to be seen.

Getting Seen

Sitting and waiting has never been my thing.

When I had my punk band we had to gig. No gigs meant and no fans. This meant gigging. This meant posters. This meant flyers and this mean time to do that stuff. It was hassle but it had to be done.

With my salon when I opened in the bigger town and went from 250 sq. ft. To over 2000 sq. ft. And in a town with 35 other salons something big had to take place. I had to be seen and had to be seen as the one and only option.

It took massive efforts. It does takes effort. It has to be done daily! Daily means every single day!

Content and doing content these days is easier than ever (and as boring as hell.) It's part of the worst advice you'll ever get as a new copywriter from a new 'expert.'

When I started writing copy you could hardly buy a book on the subject. Today, there are literally hundreds and hundreds of books on writing copy and so-called copy secrets. Mostly these books are from delusional new copywriters and those that have never written copy for real campaigns, returns, sales or higher response. It's a swamp out there now for new writers!

The fact is being a great copywriter isn't enough these days. You have to get known, get a reputation and build a group of followers that will want to pay you good money.

It's never been easier to get seen, but it's never been harder at the same time.

I see so much about SEO and getting seen online. I can tell you this after being online since 1997 SEO is as good as impossible today. The only strategy for SEO I can give is stick to the basics. I no longer give any focus to this subject.

And the same goes for most social media. I have never once had a premium clients from social media. I've had my social medias since 2007. I think that says it all.

I try never to get overly wrapped up in new strategies and just stick to what works. The endless new stuff is just a distraction. For me part of my getting known has mostly being about a few things. Branding has always been a strong part of my businesses (ff3300). Branding for positioning, power, perception and my unique flavour.

Developing a voice that sounds different to everyone else's voice and always aiming high for the big fish not just everyone and anyone. For me, that has just felt like the obvious thing to do. I don't try too hard with it and just be myself. I know that works, see what works, have seen what's failed. I stick to what I know. If I need to know more I learn it. I don't but a whole forest of books just to have a whole forest of books. For me that's pointless and debilitating.

It's tough to get known staying at home all day but you can get known by staying at home also with the web if you get smart and take a differing route to most other copywriters.

The reality and bottom-line is you have to build a reputation where you will be as good as instantly recognised for who and what you are.

I've spoken all over the globe from USA to New Zealand to get seen. I've distributed hundreds of thousands of DVD courses to be seen. I've got to know the who's who in direct marketing and made huge efforts to be known by them. I dressed and wore clothing that was branded and highly noticeable to get remembered. I worked super-hard on my web presence. My premium perspective positioning is huge. But more than anything else I created great work and that got seen by the right people.

And by the way … I invested cash. I never expected to buy a $11 eBook and get rich sitting on Facebook waiting for someone to like me. I worked out my acquisition cost per client. I took planes to meet them, ate in high-end restaurants to impress them and used my hard-earned cash to invest into my business. I rebuild my website at least twice every year. That's not free.

Once spent £500 on a dinner and almost £2,000 for the weekend just to get my client. Nothing is free.

I once flew to Switzerland to consult with a client.
I even flew into Melbourne Australia to see a client.
I made the effort and did things different.
It was and could be very hard and very fast.
It worked.
I had failures.
That's how you get seen.
Just show up for yourself.

Business Building

Money isn't always the goal.

It never has been for me. Money has no guarantees on health and happiness. For me a happy life comes first and business second. As far as I am concerned both have always been one.

Recently, I received an invite to fly to the other side of the world. I was asked to share what I know over a couple of days about strategic thinking and new ideas. I would get paid first class everything and they would also pay for my family to join me. The payment was $50,000.

I turned it down. Why? It just didn't fit in with my lifestyle in that moment. I would have loved the cash and the trip, but it felt like an intrusion on my life flow at that point of time due to just having our new baby.

Building my businesses has always paid me very well when I put the real things of life first. Those things are my family, my spiritual needs and health. Of course money has its place. Have no one and I have experienced plenty of money. I know what I prefer.

But I do have to build my businesses. We have over half a dozen in total and they all need to be worked on every week. I work hard. I rarely stop and if what I am doing isn't working I just don't do it and make the changes needed. (and of course I need time to write books like this)

The best tip I can share with you is take the route that no one else is taking to build your business. You will easily find online groups with thousands of new copywriters. Most will be hunting, tracking, chasing and waiting to a client to get in touch with them. You should avoid those places like the plague. Get creative and get creative every day.

If you are chasing fame and adoration copywriting is the wrong job.

Know what you want and pursue what you want until it arrives.

If I did it …

When To Say No…!

Not all money is good money.

You will know when to say no. You will feel when to say no. Everything inside of you will tell you something isn't right. You will just feel it.

I can tell from a single conversation of just minutes with a prospect if it is not in harmony with what I am doing. It's a skill but a skill you can learn.

If it feels wrong.

SAY NO and mean NO!

Today's Copywriters

First, let me say there are some amazing copywriters out there that I do admire. I don't know a lot about their work but I can tell and feel they have an ethic from the way the present themselves.

I would love to list them here but I would hate to miss out some so I won't list them just in case.

A huge chunk of new copywriters have been taught by 'gurus' claiming to be ace or top-flight copywriters. It seems the priority of new copywriters is to release a course of create a book copied from someone else's book.

I have met these guys and frankly they mostly leave me shocked at their attitude and poor work. I find that approach poor and abusive to a clients trust. I also find it shocking they would expect someone to invest into them.

Being a copywriter isn't just about writing. I cannot say that enough. Being a great copywriter first and foremost is about having a good, well informed, well researched and sharp mind that is relatively free from preassigned restrictions (like formulas.)

The problem with most new copywriters is this seems to be way outside their brief and they come to me for advice shocked that what they see as great copy has failed. The good news is that can be fixed. Take action to learn only from the very best. You will pay for exactly what you get.

When I train my mentor copywriters one of the first things I do with them is force them to unsubscribe from all email lists until we are done with my training.

I only allow them to buy classic books from true experts.

There is a reason for that!

That reasons is to set yourself up to win the game of copywriting right from the start.

Wanted: Great Copywriters

Despite the brilliance of A.I. writing and delivering sharp and very targeted copy and also the thousands of new copywriters now available online, there is still and will always be millions of businesses needing outstanding copywriters with smart minds.

Filling the void is critical. If you get amazing with your skills you can fill that void. I spent hours reading, studying, staying up all night and pushing an uneducated brain to become educated. I did everything I could to work with the very best rather just anyone. I pushed and used all the business tools I knew I could use and push until I had a brand that would stand out. In other words I did everything.

If you want to stand out as a great high-demand copywriter you have to push yourself hard. I did that and so can you. But … It will take superhuman effort to claim your super human copywriter status.

Tune in to what is happening in the world at all times. Finance, daily lives, trends and more. This all affects the mindset and in turn affects how you need to write copy for the current generation.

Don't forget.

I am an ex-hairdresser that did what I am talking about.

205

You can do this.

What I Learned From Accidentally Becoming A Copywriter

As you've now read it really was accidental.

I never thought about being a copywriter or writing copy. For me it was always part of the bigger picture, which in my world was all about getting results so everything can be paid for and supported. Feed my kids and pay my bills.

Higher education is a key, but not everything. I have always taken a learn as you go approach in a lot of things in my life. So many new writers these days take course after course, read book after book, subscribe to endless emails and love to sit at the back or try to steal the lead in Facebook groups. My question remains; where is the money? Everything has to be paid for right?

I spent £5 on a book by David Ogilvy and that was the key that unlocked my own door into copywriting initially. I am not saying this is the only way. But what I am saying is this; the only way is to take the amount of action needed to be taken to become what you want to become. Are you doing that?

If you want a field full of plants what you have to do plant a lot of seeds. Plant just one seed you will get just one plant and that's if it grows. The seeds you plant the more will grow and bring in a harvest.

I spent a small fortune on travelling, marketing; advertising my services but my biggest spend of all was my valuable time. Hour after hour, day after day, week and month after month learning and discovering a skill that is so valuable that once learned that skill gave me the ability to transform my life on many occasions.

There had to be a predictable outcome. Why was I taking so much trouble to walk away from a 20-year old career in hairdressing to learn something brand new? Where was it taking me and could it not only replace my income but give me a higher income?

I knew what I wanted, I was focused on what I wanted but again it come all the way back to how much was I willing to do so I can reach my outcome?

I was pushing myself massively and even now I didn't realise the effect that would have. The seeds had been planted but not all seeds grow at the same time. Some of the results from enquiries from clients were to come back to me year upon year later.

I had a new client come to me in 2012. He mentioned on the phone he saw me speak and wanted to use my services. I smiled and asked when he saw me. He told me it was early 2000. In fact it was that very same day I spoke at the jay Abraham even in London.

I learned to be patient but never give up seeing my new business.

Copy Is Conversation In Print – That's It!

As a young man, I was an ordained minister for over 20-years from 1985 to 2006. Part of my ordination was that I had a regular Bible reading schedule. Part of the schedule was to go from start to finish reading the Bible. I completed the Bible maybe six times.

The Bible has to be the greatest piece of copy ever written yet here is the thing. There are no headlines, no pre-heads, no sub-headlines, and no bullets in fact none of anything associated with modern copywriting 1,2,3 systems.

There is a compelling, curious, at times crazy, compulsive and endless stream of brilliant story telling that carries you from the start of the story through to the end time and time again.

There is even a call to action in many areas of the copy based on basic human emotions like fear and loyalty, love, jealousy and more. The Bible also reveals mastery of single word use and the power of those single words. Resurrection. Crucifixion. Passover. Archangel. God. Jesus. It also reveals how the deep embedding of single words can carry more power than a full page of words.

This just about sums up copy for me. I get asked how long should copy be, but the real reply has nothing to do with copy itself. It has more to do with; have you told the full story or emitted critical parts of the story?

The longest direct mailer I wrote was over 130 pages for a client. That mailer resulted in sales going into the millions. Was it too long or was it as long as it should be?

The real lesson in writing is having the ability to understand how a person thinks or how a human being thinks. Each marketplace is very different and each marketplace has its own reactionary triggers that create sales.

For example, it is enough for Apple to use a single number to push orders through the roof. This has been created over time using deep embedding based on the need to have the next best thing. Here are a few billion-dollar examples to prove that. iPhone 7, iPhone 7 Plus, iPhone 8, iPhone X and so on. See how brilliant they have been?

They built a story, created expectation and a thirst for the latest and best. They still use the same word … iPhone … but just add a single digit! Just brilliant.

Writing is really that easy. Most modern copywriters have fallen for the 'format' methods yet the format doesn't really exist. I have created copy many times with no headlines and no formats yet that copy has still sold and sold well.

I've seen copywriters try and create long sales pages for things like rug tape or dog food. That's just crazy!

As a hairdresser and building my salon business the biggest thing I ever discovered was what do clients think before they come to my salon? Once I found out I answered all of their existing conversations taking place in their heads. Then would write down the exact words they would be thinking when looking at themselves in the mirror when alone.

I would use those words in adverts so they felt like they were reading their own words. They would pick this up without thought and then attach themselves to that very conversation. This was the trigger that had the client saying to themselves, "they are talking about me", "that is me", "they get it I will go there" and so forth.

The other thing I want to talk about is the myth of persuasion. Persuasion can only ever have an outcome of regret because they really didn't buy for the reasons that they genuinely require or need the product. If you have to work your brains out to persuade and then finally get the sale it really isn't a sale worth having.

Choosing the right words is critical. If you say the right thing, but use the wrong word you won't be able to connect with the reader. For example, years ago I wrote and advised for a golf company. They loved the work but I had made one critical mistake. (as I wasn't a golfer, but I also failed to research properly)

"Alan we love the copy but we have changed one word. You use the word 'sand-pit' but the word we use in the industry is actually 'bunker' so we changed it".

Simple mistake but mistakes that took me away from the conversation of the reader and would likely have reduced response.

So many times I've seen single words make such a huge difference to reaction and response.

It is always worth the time - regardless of length of the copy you've written to choose the precise words to use in any copy.

And life now?

Life Today for The Accidental Copywriter

Life is wonderful.

I've serviced some huge clients. The most famous hairdressing salons in England and Scotland. The biggest house rental company in the U.K. A huge security company, multi-million pound turnover organisations and even small struggling start-ups. My business types go into the hundreds and I've loved it. But they all take masses of my time.

Today, time is the most precious of things for me. I don't think managing time is my greatest gift so I like to make the most of what I manage to manage.

At 57-years and have just experienced a true miracle and become a father for the 5th time to my darling boy and son Demna. I live between the vibrantly rich and creative Manchester in the U.K. and power-house and very bohemian Tbilisi, the capital of The Republic of Georgia. I like to appreciate and enjoy all of these things. That takes my time. Sometimes I like to take one-way tickets to Tbilisi and fly back when we are ready. I love to be able to live like that.

I start everyday with coffee at our local coffee shop of choice. I go to the gym at least three times each week and try and hit yoga at least once.

My life values are no longer in the materiality of things. I don't really drive cars that much so have no need for expensive cars. I don't need to live in a mansion and enjoy our perfectly small home. I don't chase or worship money as money guarantees nothing in life. I still get paid huge amounts for creating huge amounts. That's the way things are. It's the perfect exchange of value.

Everything still has to be paid for, but I really don't write copy for just anyone that pays me anymore. I am only interested in interesting projects. They must partner and pay me well for me to give me hard-earned skills into the time to create and write. I consult, fix and repair businesses of all sizes on a regular basis. I really only work with serious business builders these days.

I like to work from Monday to Wednesday. I usually wind down at around 2pm each day. I deliver at least a months worth of work in that time. The rest of the week I like to take things as they arrive. I always write daily. I write in my phone, on my computer, in pads and in my head. A day will never pass without me writing. These are my seeds for the future.

As I write this book, I am working on a movie based on one of my books. I have just finished a screenplay for a BBC TV pilot show. This book is my

20th published book. My life feels as though it is just wonderful.

I still have www.OrangeBeetle.com. I still have www.SalonPunk.com. www.MasterAndMan.com is one of my latest projects. I am training and mentoring writers and authors. I also publish authors and of course my own books.

I have the most beautiful wife and new son that give me so much happiness I cannot even find enough paper to express that happiness on.

This year I have been invited to give a prestigious TEDX talk. I am thrilled. Writing and writing copy was an accidental discovery that changed everything about my life. If I hadn't fallen upon writing copy and making copy work I wonder how my life would be? Older, but maybe still cutting hair?

There is more to come and more happening. For me, life is every bit the empty book that we should fill. I am trying to fill mine the very best I can and leave at least something behind to share with and help others.

Life has taught me many things. What we have right here and right now we have created. I created my life, I created the things I don't like and the things I love in my life. There is an invisible force out there that drives thoughts into a reality. I know, I have seen it happen so many times.

Never forget that thoughts really do become things if we nurture and grow those thoughts.

If you want to create a life as a writer you must ask yourself why? Why are you doing this? Writing can give you everything but it can also give you nothing.

It is up to you to create everything. Are you ready to do that?

I was a hairdresser for over twenty years and I made the huge change into a new career in my early forties.

You can become a copywriter if that is what you really want.

I truly hope this little book gives you the belief that if copywriting is a future you really want for yourself it is possible. It does take hard and determined work but the rewards are just amazing.

If it worked for me - Alan the hairdresser - surely it can work for you.

Thank you for giving me your time and reading this book.

The Accidental Copywriter.

Alan Forrest Smith

The Only Tips I Will Offer New Copywriters

Believe you can do this. The mind makes things possible or impossible.

Don't do it just for the money - that rarely works - you have to love doing this stuff.

Get a mentor for learning the shortcuts and avoiding the time loss.

Don't join email lists and online groups - for now.

Write everyday - and never miss a day for at least the first year.

Limit your reading library. Too much information creates confusion. Focus on one or two greats to emulate.

Think more and write less. Copy doesn't start on the page it begins in your mind.

You will need time to learn. Steal back time from TV and useless time sucking pursuits.

Be honest and ethical. It's ok to turn away certain industries and work even when the pay-check can be huge.

Understand your value. Your work can generate millions in sales. It's a crazy thing to accept a few hundred in payment when their reward is so great.

If you cannot get started yourself get a job with an agency. This is a great place to find your way.

Invest into yourself and your future. What you spend on this isn't the important bit. The important bit is where it will lead you and is it to a place you want to be?

Practice higher response methods. If you know something works, find out why and copy it where you can copy it. Apple sell tons of tech with short copy. Why? Find out.

Movies posters (my love) sell more than anything. Why? How? Study them.

Learn as much as you can about the human condition. Once you know how people think in any marketplace that marketplace will be opened to you.

Understand copy isn't about a set structure. It doesn't have to have headline, sub-headline, bullets, offer, bonus etc. This is a myth. In some sectors that copy will fail. Find out if you need just one word or 5,000 words.

Don't take life too seriously but be serious when working with your clients.

Love your clients and treat them with respect. This also means loving the prospects. Don't disrespect humans by lying ands scheming. Karma loves a bitch and will pay you back at some point.

Be honest.

Be truthful.

Be ethical.

Set your standards.

Understand life and what makes life great.

Be the very best you can be at all times.

Never forget there is something out there much bigger than you. Invisible, visible, knowing, unknowing. It is there and it is watching. Be respectful and open.

Love people.

A Eulogy for Clayton Makepeace

As I was coming to the end of this book my friend and the the greatest copywriter I have ever known - Clayton Makepeace died. I have to say I found the announcement shocking.

Only last week I had messaged him for some words on this book. I didn't realise how ill he had become. What a huge loss.

And this is a strange thing for me to add into this book, but I just felt like I wanted to drop it in here.

Clayton's 'quick start copywriting system' is the greatest manual I have ever seen in print for a copywriter. In fact I was going to create my own manual at one time, but after I bought his I realised I could never create anything as great so I didn't bother.

The following is a small eulogy I posted for him after his death.

The Eulogy for Clayton Makepeace.

On his Facebook posts Clayton makepeace could sound like an antagonistic shit. He said what he felt and would happily write what he thought.

But that was Facebook.

I don't really have a lot of heroes in the world of writing copy. Clayton was one of them and he was right at the top.

I loved his work. I don't think I've seen a copywriter alive that could write like him. His words reflected his brilliant clever well-thought-out mind. His style was uniquely Clayton Makepeace. His approach the most cleverly direct I've seen in a modern day writer. Unmatched!

Anyone that knew John Caples will be feeling like our living Caples has just died.

One day I received a message on Facebook. To my surprise it was Clayton. We chatted about two shared loves. Motorbikes and guitars. He liked Harley, I liked old school Brit bobbers. Not long after I received a parcel through the mail It was from Clayton. It contained a couple of collectors Harley Davidson T-shirts for me. I loved that little act of connecting.

We never met but our conversations continued and to be honest I felt like I knew him as a like-minded soul passing through Earth in search of more than meaning to life.

He was a giant in this industry. His big manual is without a doubt the greatest copywriters manual I have ever seen. Thank you for sharing it Clayton. In fact it is so brilliant I try and keep it a secret.

But life runs out and his ran out. Time runs out and his ran out. The final breath leaves the body and what remains moves on. Clayton Makepeace moved on yet if you want to really know about a true Goliath of one industry he was that.

He once sent me a message that said, " Alan, there is a room here with your name on it, come anytime". He didn't really know me or I him but it always felt good to know him.

Clayton Makepeace your work helped me during a time of life crisis. I wish I had told you that. I wish we had ridden out together like we discussed. I wish we'd had fight over a fire on the road. I wish I had taken the offer to visit you.

But life is like that.

Birth, life and death.

It isn't long enough.

What a legacy.

What a giant.

What a man.

You are one of those that has left a space that I doubt will be filled. It will always be a gap that says, "Clayton Makepeace used to sit here - stay away!.

Sleep well big man.

If there is another side send a Harley to pull up outside my house and rev the engine as loud it it can be so I know you're there.

What a desperately sad announcement.

The Death of Clayton Makepeace.

April 13th 1952 - March 25th 2020

His flesh and big presence will be missed, but if you are a copywriter he left behind possibly one of the greatest legacy for copywriters you will ever find.

Clayton Makepeace what a copywriting hero in this world.

My Tiny Reading List

This is my library. You will find bigger and better. Not a huge list but this list was enough to change my life through informed education.

The Bible: (This is the first book I ever read. Maybe that is why it is the first book that changed my life entirely)

AUTHOR: GOD

Ogilvy: (this book was the second book to change my life. It was also the second book I read in full)

AUTHOR: David Ogilvy

AND …

How to Write a Good Advertisement [Paperback]

AUTHOR: VICTOR SCHWAB

Tested Advertising Methods (Prentice Hall Business Classics) [Paperback]

AUTHOR: JOHN CAPLES

Sales Letters That Sizzle: All the Hooks, Lines and Sinkers You'll Ever Need to Close Sales [Hardcover]

AUTHOR: HERSCHELL GORDON LEWIS

The Art of Writing Copy [Paperback]

AUTHOR: HERSCHELL GORDON LEWIS

Words that Sell, Revised and Expanded Edition: The Thesaurus to Help You Promote Your Products, Services, and Ideas [Paperback]

AUTHOR: RICHARD BAYAN

Phrases That Sell: The Ultimate Phrase Finder to Help You Promote Your Products, Services, and Ideas [Paperback]

AUTHOR: RICHARD BAYAN

The Copywriter's Handbook: A Step-by-step Guide to Writing Copy That Sells [Paperback]

AUTHOR: ROBERT BLY

How to Make Your Advertising Make Money [Paperback]

(VERY RARE)

AUTHOR: JOHN CAPLES

Advertising Ideas

(I PAID £200 FOR MINE... RARE)

AUTHOR: JOHN CAPLES

The Ultimate Sales Letter

AUTHOR: Dan Kennedy (anything by Kennedy is usually good)

Guerrilla Marketing: Cutting-edge strategies for the 21st century [Paperback]

AUTHOR: JAY CONRAD LEVINSON

Quick-Start Copywriting System

This is my only modern day insert. Why? This manual is a work of an advertising genius. It is also a manual that every copywriter should own. Just brilliant, just an absolutely brilliant addition to your library. Note: Hard to get hold of, I paid around $700 I think. Worth every last penny.

AUTHOR: CLAYTON MAKEPEACE

Mentor, Alliance or Partner with Alan Forrest Smith

Recently I increased one of my client's business turnover by 223.7% in under 21-days. I also took another client's business to sales of over £300,000 online from a standing start. And I recently gave a client an extra 43% in new business in a single week. And I want to share one more from a client that went from a new business to over £12,000,000 a year.

After reading this little book I think you'll get that. Over the years my sales for clients at every level have gone well into the tens of millions. I am always open to projects where we can create a value share that we are both happy with. This would be agreed only after a consultation.

I am also open to some incredible writing copy for bigger projects. And for those that need more edge, bigger ideas, breakthrough angles and proven higher response writing. And of course powerful, higher responding stories.

If you'd like to work with me you can come to me with an amazing offer, but it will have to be an offer I just cannot refuse. Your offer should involve a big picture and overview of the project. You must be solvent. You must have a budget in place. You must be opened minded. You must have a grasp of what marketing really is.

All of my work involves a downpayment, monthly residual, commissions and bonuses of sorts.

Do you need a business or copy writing mentor? Most of my new copywriters that come through a mentor program have both clients and cash in the bank. I have a very strong track record working with copywriters and those that need a proven mentor. You will find details on my sites under my mentor pages.

And my websites, I can be found for
- Writing
- Mentoring
- Speaking
- Consulting
- Creative Partnerships

Here at

www.OrangeBeetle.com
www.MasterAndMan.com
www.AlanForrestSmith.com

Bibliography

- Escape from Zoomanity
- Deliberate Recreation
- Happiness
- The Salon Punk
- Salon Extreme 21
- The Missing Client Kit
- Salon Sampler
- Observations 2008-2010
- Love Poems
- Letters from a Broken Man
- The Little Angel and The Last Christmas
- Life Why Do You Tease Me
- I Am God Have You Forgotten Me?
- I Am Bastard I Am War
- I Am Bastard I Am War (Georgian translation)
- The Accidental Copywriter

All of my books can be found on my own websites or most online bookstore.

Special Bonus For You

As a very special bonus I have put as many as I could find from my old salon ads and some letters going back as far as 1991. These are the same ads I talk about in this book.

Enjoy.

www.OrangeBeetle.com/accidentalsalonads

Lightning Source UK Ltd.
Milton Keynes UK
UKHW021823130622
404364UK00007B/1028